INTIMACY

The longing of every human heart

INTIMACY

The longing of every human heart

Terry Hershey

HARVEST HOUSE PUBLISHERS
Eugene, Oregon 97402

INTIMACY: The Longing of Every Human Heart

Copyright © 1984 by Terry Hershey
Published by Harvest House Publishers
Eugene, Oregon 97402

Library of Congress Catalog Card Number 84-61349
ISBN 0-89081-626-3

To my father,
Jerry Hershey,
who teaches me that
life is simple.

Table of Contents

Preface

1 A Culture of the Restless   3

2 Intimacy: The Illusion—Or What It Is Not   11

3 What Is Intimacy?   21

4 Obstacles to Intimacy   31

5 Where Do Our Masks Lead?   39

6 Interdependence: A Move Towards Freedom   51

7 Who Owns Me?   61

8 Intimacy With God   77

9 Slaves in a Free World   93

10 Intimate Marriages: Have We Settled for Less?   109

11 What Will Intimacy Cost Me?   125

12 Conflict: Who Needs It?   145

13 Where Do I Go from Here?
   Steps to an Intimate Lifestyle   159

14 Where Do I Go from Here?
   The Journey Continues   171

Epilogue   187

May this book be a comfort to those who are discomfortable and a discomfort to those who are comfortable.

Intimacy: Where Do I Go to Find Love?

Astory is told of a small town that was perched on the edge of a mountain. The winding road which led to the town came very close to the mountain edge at certain spots. One corner which was especially difficult to negotiate became the scene of many unfortunate accidents as cars plunged over the embankment and landed some five hundred feet below. Some people survived; others were not so fortunate.

"We need to do something about that corner," the town council proclaimed. The people of the town agreed, and the task of raising funds for the project began. It wasn't long before sufficient funds were raised and the project was on its way to completion. What did the townspeople build with their money? A hospital at the bottom of the embankment.

We go through life much like that little town did. Faced with obstacles and danger points in our own lives, we respond by raising funds. We gather our available energies and build hospitals in anticipation of our accidents. The lesson is clear: dealing only with the symptoms and the consequences keeps us from addressing the real problem.

Certainly "hospitals" are necessary. Regardless of the extent of prevention, casualties do occur. An earlier book, *Beginning Again: Life After a Relationship Ends*, discusses that reality. We need to know where to turn after a casualty has occurred or, in terms of the Good Samaritan parable, we may find ourselves lying in the ditch watching people pass us by. Although many may go past us without stopping to bandage our wounds, one Healer will always stop. Our loving God is in the business of binding wounds. Jesus made that clear when He declared His mission:

> The Spirit of the Lord is on me,
> > because he has anointed me to preach good news to the poor.
> He has sent me to proclaim freedom for the prisoners
> > and recovery of sight for the blind,
> to release the oppressed,
> > to proclaim the year of the Lord's favor.
>
> *Luke 4:18-19*

These words offer comfort and hope as we live in a world of personal and relational casualties where pain is very real. Were it not for hospitals at the bottom of the hills in our lives— were it not for friends, family, and significant others— we would not be where we are today.

But I do not and cannot believe that we are destined to a life of repeated hospital admittance. Instead we must learn to address the symptoms before they become critical. The possibility of successfully negotiating those mountain curves offers us the hope of reaching the top of the mountain safely. We must believe that, along the way, there are materials available for building guardrails and warning signs to guide us along this journey of life.

This is a book about intimacy—a mysterious something that for many of us seems to exist at the top of a mountain that we will never be able to climb. If you want easy answers about making that climb and reaching a point of intimacy, this book will disappoint you. I don't have easy answers because I am still struggling with the subject in my own life and relationships. Whenever you write a book, you run the risk of implicitly declaring yourself an expert on a given topic. Experts, however, are dull people. They cease to grow as they strive to maintain the image of their expertise. So let me say at the start that I am not an expert. Why, then, write the book? I suppose there are three reasons:

1. I know what it is like to be a casualty of intimacy. I have been at the bottom of the valley. I have seriously questioned whether intimacy is worth the effort or whether intimacy is even a possibility for me. I write this book to affirm that the bottom of the valley is not the end of the world. The painful plunge over the edge of the cliff does not forever eliminate the possibility of reaching mountain heights. In fact, our casualties (our mistakes, our accidents, and our failures) can be our schoolmasters. They offer us lessons to be learned. "He who has ears," Jesus often said, "let him hear." In the same vein, he who desires to grow, to be whole, to gain maturity, and to experience intimacy, let him or her listen carefully to the voice of personal pain.

2. I have not only been at the bottom, but, in the words of Martin Luther King, "I've been to the mountaintop . . ." as well. Two significant people have risked their hearts with me, and this book will talk about those relationships and the mountaintop moments which they offered me. These glimpses of intimacy have taught me, among other things, that intimacy is possible and that intimacy is worth the high cost.

Just as King's dream spurred him on even in the face of adversity, my dreams spur me on. If this book can awaken in you that dream, then it was worth writing. If this book can paint for you an encouraging picture of a journey toward intimacy, then it has achieved its goal.

3. Finally, I write this book to make you think and to help you act. Just as ingredients remain useless until they are stirred, so also with us. Our yearning for comfort often keeps us from attempting any climb, from shooting for any goal, or from beginning any journey.

It is my prayer, therefore, that this book will stir us up—that it will raise more questions than we can now answer. I hope it creates in each of us a desire to know more, a desire to not settle for mediocrity, a desire to seek out the abundant life Jesus spoke of, and a desire to understand ourselves and our capacity for intimacy. May this book be a comfort to those who are discomfortable and a discomfort to those who are comfortable.

Intimacy is not a new subject. Many writers have preceded me, and many will come after. In fact, I intend to draw from the wisdom of those who have come before me. While this book is not the only word, neither is it the final word. It can only be a personal word. And that is what it shall be—a word about a life-long struggle on the journey toward intimacy. It's a journey of joy and pain, highs and lows, laughter and tears, risks and rejections. It's the journey of one who desires to know what it means to be fully alive.

There is in all of us a sense of incompleteness that can only be eased when we are in relationship with other people.

CHAPTER ONE

A Culture of the Restless

I frequently spend time at a monastery in the high desert area of Southern California. I go there for time alone, for study, and for writing. Right now, sitting at this table in the monastery, I can look out the window of my room as the sun sets beyond the local foothills of the San Gabriel Mountains. The hues of blue, red, and orange make the sky far more entertaining than any television program could be. Only fifteen yards from my desk and chair, rabbits and quail vie for any grass that remains on a small patch of dry ground. The scene offers a peaceful change from my normal activity.

Lest my description cause you to give up your current vocation for monastic life, let me share the flip side of my monastery experience. Though I have been here several times, it never really gets any easier. One of my journal entries explains: "It is difficult to calculate what one learns. I came on a retreat to learn and grow—but what do I have to show for my efforts? We are always needing to prove ourselves, our worth, and the significance—the usefulness—of our time. Maybe I am afraid to say that I was alone with God—period. It is peaceful here—at least externally. Why, then, is that inner peace of the soul so difficult to find?" This sense of restlessness, as uncomfortable as it can be, reminds

3

me again and again that I want a home—a place where my soul can find peace and where I can find peace about who I am.

This restlessness is fostered by the world in which we live. Each of us feels the need to protect ourselves, and we become restless under this pressure to secure ourselves, our families, and even those possessions which we value. This need to protect is based on the possibility that someone may take away what we have. I need, therefore, either to hide what I have from you or else make it inaccessible: either way, I quickly develop defense mechanisms. This attitude of protectionism has in fact pervaded our relationships in the same way that it has defined our national security. Our culture is full of individuals who have spent enormous amounts of energy and time and maybe even money on personal defense systems, always with the intention of protecting themselves from intruders.

"But is that all wrong?" you ask. "Is not an element of caution important in relationships? Must I throw caution to the wind?"

There is no doubt in my mind that such questions are both legitimate and important. The issue, however, is one of focus. Consider this question: which is worse—being personally violated or the *fear* of being personally violated? Neither is better than the other. The fear, however, can preoccupy us and inhibit the growth of intimate relationships. If I am consumed by my need to protect myself, for instance, then I view everyone around me as a potential threat—and you'll have little chance of getting to me if you need to work your way through several layers of defense!

What do the lack of inner peace I felt at the monastery and this need to protect myself have in common? They both stem from a sense of restlessness, a sense of not being at home with myself or with other people. Tension arises from the conflict between wanting to know myself and share myself and still wanting to protect myself. Why do we struggle with

4

this sense of restlessness? What is it that continues to cause this anxiety? Why do we seem to be people who are uncomfortable with who we are?

To begin answering these questions, let us consider the issue of intimacy. Without even defining the word, we know that intimacy is something we desire. There is in all of us a sense of incompleteness that can only be eased when we are in relationship with other people. At the same time, these thoughts of relationships which offer fulfillment often serve to remind us of our restlessness; thoughts of relationships often serve to remind us of how alone we feel.

In order not to be reminded of that sense of being homeless and of not belonging, we frantically search for something that will provide a reprieve from restlessness. In today's culture, we can look various places for that peace which comes when we feel as if we belong. Some of these options are legitimate, but even then we often seek them and need them for the wrong reasons.

- Many see *marriage* as a haven from restlessness, and for a period of months—maybe even years—that can be true. But it doesn't take long before my hope that my spouse can provide a real home and genuine peace for my soul begins to cause strain in the relationship. Sooner or later, my wife falls short of my expectations and my original restlessness is even more intense. At that point, my anger is, of course, directed at my spouse: "Why were you unable to be for me what I needed? Why were you unable to take away my restlessness?"

- Many people find a sense of security in the *bar scene*. As one woman said, "I want to meet people. I'm tired of bars, but it's the only way I know." I believe that the popularity of bars (currently our cultural watering hole) is, first and foremost, evidence of our hunger to belong and therefore is also a reflection of the universal sense of personal restlessness. Unfortunately, though, by their

5

very nature, bars only tend to perpetuate restlessness. One-night encounters, over-the-bar counseling, evaluating people merely on appearances and superficial conversation—this bar scene inevitably comes up short in its unspoken promises to offer some kind of belonging and some relief for our restlessness.

- Finding the bar scene unthinkable or at least unappealing, some people view the *church* as a watering hole of sorts. The setting is the "fellowship hall" where we conduct rituals called "coffee hours." Obviously, in churches we are confronted with the reality of restless people. The need for fellowship programs is, therefore, entirely legitimate. The problem lies in the fact that our instant-answer culture seeks to create immediate solutions to such problems as loneliness. The unspoken promises that church programs will create instant or solid community can only disappoint. If we expect instant but genuine fellowship—if we are told that community is supposed to magically take place during a given hour—we strive for belonging, immediacy, and closeness at the expense of sharing real emotion and honest concerns.

- Believing that there is no real solution to restlessness, many people opt for *personal isolation*. "All of my attempts at community and friendship seem to fail, so why even try?" is a common attitude. Ironically and sadly, people often maintain a facade of social involvement while internally they are emotionally and spiritually isolated. They do not necessarily believe that their restlessness will simply disappear, but they do hope that their isolation will not add to their inner tension or disturb their shaky sense of self. By isolating themselves, these people avoid any movement forward; they avoid any movement of risk and relationship.

As these four options suggest, we are not at all comfortable with our sense of restlessness. In fact, I believe that we are

6

afraid of this feeling—so afraid that we are preoccupied with it. Paradoxically, Americans spend enormous amounts of time, energy, and money cultivating this very sense of restlessness. Tim Hansel expressed it with this thought: "We worship our work, we play at worship, and we work at our play."[1] We are continually creating new toys to occupy us during our free time. We return from vacation time more tired and stressed than when we left.

What underlies our lack of inner peace, our frantic search for community, and our intense efforts to play? I believe it is the fact that *we are afraid to be alone with ourselves*. We are not able to live peaceably "at home" with ourselves. We also find ourselves dealing with the fear that our sense of self—however well-defined it is or isn't—and our inner life—however peaceful it may or may not be—will somehow be taken away from us. With that fear, we convince ourselves that even a shaky house is better than no house at all! So we work diligently to protect whatever sense of self we already have. We strive for security and comfort; we desperately seek inner peace.

In our journey toward intimacy, we must begin here, right where we are. We must acknowledge our restlessness—and this acknowledgment is difficult because it is unsettling. It rocks the boat as it forces us to recognize our vulnerability—as it forces me to look squarely at my fragile self. Growth, however, can only begin when there is such a confession. Again, this confession is simply the honest acknowledgment of where we are. It does not pretend that we are something other than emotional orphans in search of a home. In failing to acknowledge our situation, though, we choose, in effect, to play God: we deny any need for assistance on our journey to wholeness.

Change—the movement toward wholeness—begins with a sense of need. That sense of need comes with the recognition of our insecurity and inadequacy. The step of confession, as I define it, is the crucial act of recognition that allows us to begin the journey. Neither you nor I need to pretend that we are further along than we are. My journey, for instance, begins as I acknowledge where I am right now. If I am unwilling to honestly acknowledge my need, I am destined to continue my pursuit of immediate and temporary means of pacifying my restlessness; I may be on the unhealthy path of eventually repressing the fact that there is any need at all.

Still, the fact remains that each of us desperately desires inner peace, a sense of belonging, the ability to reach out and trust another person—every one of us restless, homeless beings does desire intimacy. Before we look more closely at this thing called "intimacy," consider what St. Augustine wrote to God: "Our hearts are restless until they find their rest in Thee." As you search for an emotional home, look first to God your Creator. Ask Him for His peace, His presence, and His guidance as you travel on your journey toward intimacy.

...intimacy is not a destination or a possession or a status. Intimacy is a journey.

CHAPTER TWO

Intimacy: The Illusion—
Or What It Is Not

Ellen sat motionless in the chair across from me. She stared silently at the floor of my office. We had been discussing age and the threat it became as the years passed. Ellen was afraid of becoming old.

Finally she spoke. "I don't want to be old," she said.

"Are you aware of any reasons for those feelings?" I probed.

"No one will love me. It is hard to love an old person. When I die, I want someone to be loving me. I want to know inside that it was worth my while being here. I want someone to tell me that I am significant. I want to matter to someone." The tears came to Ellen's eyes. She had touched the heart of the matter.

As I've said, without even defining "intimacy," we all know that we want it. We want to leave life with more than just an epitaph that reads, "Here lies the body of John R. Doe. He once filled space on the earth below." We all want to be loved. We all want to feel significant.

This desire for intimacy, however, does not automatically assure us that we know what intimacy is. In fact, I believe that most of us have been fooled by certain myths about intimacy. Swallowing hook, line, and sinker a cultural definition of intimacy, we spend our days on a journey that has no destination. Before we understand what intimacy is, then, let's be very clear about what intimacy is not.

1. Intimacy is not marriage.

Though most of us are sophisticated enough to realize that magic is only an illusion that exists solely in our minds, we continue to believe that the marriage ceremony involves a kind of magic. It is as if the words "I do" serve as the wave of a magic wand over the heads of the new couple. It is as if these two words bestow on the bride and groom certain qualities that were not theirs before—one such quality being the ability to be intimate. In other words, we assume that intimacy comes with marital vows: I pledge you my love and receive intimacy in return.

I think we have been conned. Marriage does not and cannot guarantee intimacy. Yes, marital relations are to be characterized by intimacy, but it is naive to assume that intimacy is guaranteed by the vows. Why? Because assuming the presence of intimacy is a thought rather than an action—and intimacy requires effort and work. As with any journey, the path to intimacy requires action, not just talk. You can't avoid that effort with the shortcut called "marriage": "I do" cannot mean "I've arrived."

2. Intimacy is not sexual intercourse.

When two persons have had a sexual encounter, it is usually described by the statement, "We were intimate with one another." Perhaps. If I have had sex with you, however, I may or may not have been intimate with you. Instead, as we'll talk about in chapter 9, sex often becomes a barrier to intimacy. In fact, many people find themselves wondering why relationships they are in seem to be deteriorating even though there is an active sex life. I frequently talk with men and women who have been "getting it on" but have come nowhere close to sharing anything intimate.

This emptiness can happen, for instance, when sex is seen as a possession and a guarantee of intimacy. Such an attitude turns sex into a placebo for overcoming any ill which might threaten the relationship. This truth was confirmed in a conversation I had with Bill and Edna. Bill had just finished telling me how significant their relationship had become.

"Tell me about your ability to communicate," I said.

"We understand each other completely," Edna replied.

"What about the times when there is conflict, when you don't agree, or when there is misunderstanding?" I asked the question, assuming that all was not as good as it seemed.

"There is very little conflict in our relationship." Bill spoke hesitantly as if he were asking Edna's permission to make such a statement.

Edna went on: "Yes. Whenever there's a disagreement, we've definitely learned the art of making up!" They both laughed.

"That sounds good," I offered, "but I want to make sure I understand." I continued to follow my instincts about Bill and Edna. "I'm assuming that you have a fairly active sex life."

"Yes, we do!" Bill jumped in. "Sex couldn't be better for either of us." Again, he seemed to look to Edna for confirmation.

I went on. "Undoubtedly there are times when one of you gets irritated or upset with the other—you know, when little things go wrong . . ."

They nodded as if to say, "Sure, of course."

"My hunch is that you find sex a good way to smooth over those rough spots. I suspect, too, that you have found sex a good way to avoid talking about how you really feel. You probably even talk about the fact that you're glad you 'love' each other enough to make up so effectively. I suspect that

13

sex has become a substitute for talking. When you run out of things to say or when you are afraid to express your hurt or anger, you assume that you can always have sex. Your assumption seems to be that sex is a strong enough bond for an intimate relationship."

I had taken a risk by being so blunt, but their somber faces told the story: I was right. Fortunately, Bill and Edna were willing to listen, so I continued.

"None of us can use a sexual relationship as a guarantee of intimacy. The two are not necessarily synonomous. When sex is used to cover up real emotions, to prevent risking real communication, or to avoid conflict, then sex is trivialized. It becomes a magic pill or security blanket. When we understand that sex is not intimacy but instead that intimacy is a foundation for a healthy sexual relationship, then sex recovers its dignity and sanctity."

Still, too many of us assume that going to bed with someone makes us intimate. That is tantamount to saying that putting a violin in your hands makes you a Stradivari or Isaac Stern. You must have what it takes to be a violinist in order for the violin to be transformed from a meaningless (although perhaps beautiful) object to a source of musical beauty and power. In the same way, our bodies are not automatic tickets to intimacy. Only when sexual intercourse is shared in a context of intimacy is there true beauty and unifying power.

3. Intimacy is not found only in a relationship with a member of the opposite sex.

When people hear the word "intimate," they generally think of the opposite sex. First, this way of thinking reinforces the previous myths that intimacy is found in sexual relations or in marriage. This way of thinking also robs people of one of life's richest experiences—an intimate relationship with a member of the same sex.

14

As I write these words, I think of my friend Roy. Through the years he has taught me many lessons about openness, honesty, and friendship. He has encouraged me through difficult times, and he has allowed me to be myself. I took the risk: I gave a little of myself away and I found a friend—an intimate *male* friend—in return.

4. Intimacy is not measured merely on frequency of contact.

A young man in my office declared his plan to marry a woman whom he had known for one month. In his defense, he argued, "But we've been together twenty-nine of the last thirty evenings. I believe that I know her better than most people who have been dating much longer know each other."

What he said may be true—but not necessarily. Assuming that frequent contact insures intimacy is misunderstanding intimacy. Two observations need to be noted here: a) It is not merely the amount of contact which is significant. It is what we do with the contact that determines whether the time is a building block for intimacy. b) Lest my first point sound like an argument for "quality versus quantity of time" in relationships, let me assure you that nothing provides a substitute for time—lots of time. Twenty-nine days do not a mature and intimate relationship make. Yes, seeds of intimacy can be planted, but the watering, the fertilizing, and the weeding take months and years.

Acknowledging these false ideas we've just looked at is important because they can seriously distort our understanding of intimacy and consequently thwart our attempt to live lives of intimacy. All four ideas assume that intimacy is achieved by virtue of a certain status, whether it be the status of marriage, the status of a sexual relationship, the status of a relationship with the opposite sex (probably a dating relationship), or the status of a relationship of frequent contact.

15

What is the problem with equating intimacy with a certain status? Intimacy is no longer a goal. Instead, a particular status is the goal. This brings up one more statement about what intimacy is not.

5. Intimacy is not a plateau.

At the conclusion of one of my recent seminars, a woman came to me and sighed, "Is it ever possible to reach intimacy? How long did it take before you became intimate?"

The question is a red herring: it distracts attention from what intimacy really is because it is built on myth. "Reaching intimacy" implies, first, that intimacy is a plateau which a person attains someday and, second, that this plateau is probably reserved for the "relational elite." This statement, like the other four, speaks of intimacy as a status. Once a person achieves this status, there will no longer be any need for self-evaluation or for effort. The journey will be considered complete and intimacy will be thought of as a possession to guard.

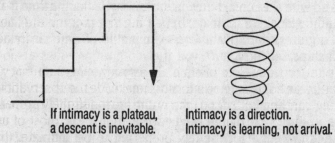

If intimacy is a plateau, a descent is inevitable.

Intimacy is a direction. Intimacy is learning, not arrival.

Furthermore, striving toward the status of intimacy can lead to competition. As I climb a staircase or ladder with the view that I need to arrive at a certain rung or level if I am to find success—if I am to find intimacy—I begin to envy others who seem to be farther up the ladder than I am. I also feel guilty that I am not farther along. My energy becomes entirely focused on achieving a status.

What I fail to realize is that when my energy is focused on a status ("When I get married . . .," for example) my energy becomes entirely focused on myself. My energy is no longer focused on our relationship. My relationship with you simply becomes a means to an end—the end being becoming intimate. You become merely an object that assists me in my climb up the ladder. You (and other people as well) become dispensable: it is more important for me to become intimate than it is for me to know you. People become rungs on the ladder I'm climbing to intimacy. Even with this strategy, intimacy seems to elude me: it always seems to be out there or around the next corner. Intimacy always seems to be on the next rung or atop the next plateau. Intimacy never seems attainable.

Furthermore, suppose that such a ladder could be climbed or such a plateau reached. I believe that this moment of "I've arrived" would be the moment when a person begins his or her descent. If the "I do" of the marriage vows means to me "I am intimate," I will no longer work toward intimacy. No more effort means no more progress on the journey. Lack of movement means lack of growth; it means stagnation and death. If I am not moving and not growing, I can hardly be experiencing life—I can hardly be experiencing intimacy.

How, then, do we approach our journey toward intimacy? Swiss psychologist Paul Tournier once made the observation that "many people spend their entire life indefinitely preparing to live."[1] The same is true in relationships: most of us spend our time indefinitely preparing to be intimate. (In reality, most of us spend our time indefinitely preparing for intimacy to be given to us—and that is not how intimacy works!) We need not approach intimacy so doubtfully. We can approach the journey with certainty—beginning with a clear understanding of what intimacy isn't. This step involves being honest with ourselves about the excess baggage—the misunderstandings about intimacy—that we are carrying. When we are able to acknowledge and then discard our false ideas, we are free to learn, to grow, and to give. I will be free to love you. The intimacy which we experience and enjoy on the journey of life will be a precious by-product of our relationship rather than the very focus of our lives.

Let me say again, then, that intimacy is not a destination or a possession or a status. Intimacy is a journey. The issue, then, is not where or when we arrive somewhere. The issue is learning to love the journey—the journey of intimacy which is the journey of life.

I believe that the very hope we have for intimacy indicates our capacity to experience intimacy.

CHAPTER THREE

What Is Intimacy?

I recall standing in the streets of San Francisco where I had gone with a friend for the weekend. I had been struggling to understand what was happening in my life. I was sure that something was missing. I had just gone through a divorce, and the jungle of "single adult life" was very confusing to me. Furthermore, dealing with my failure in a relationship was aggravating my sense of worthlessness. Although I wanted to be all that God wanted me to be—I wanted to be fully alive—I had turned my life into a fortress and had locked the door. And *no one* was going to get in and hurt me.

Oh, yes, I would throw prayers over the wall of the fortress and say, "God, help me to know what to do"; "God, help me get my life straightened out"; and even "God, send that blonde through the door with a battering ram and let her carry me away." But never did I invite God or anyone else inside that fortress with me. Why? Because I was too afraid.

For me, the very desire for intimacy was a source of tension: I desperately wanted to experience intimacy at the same time that I desperately feared it. I knew that something in my life was missing. I knew, too, that I wanted that something. I believed that this something would make me whole and complete. And yet, at the same time, this very longing

21

caused the deepest fears, the sharpest anxieties, and the strongest barriers to arise. And I couldn't sort it out. The feelings I was wrestling with are common to all of us. *Each one of us desires closeness at the same time that we protect ourselves from it.*

As I think of my weekend in San Francisco and where I was emotionally at that time, I see that I knew of intimacy by virtue of its absence. The vacuum within made me hope for intimacy, and this hope indicated a capacity for intimacy. Still, the desire for intimacy remained in tension with my fears and with the haunting question, "What, after all, is this elusive thing called 'intimacy'?" One way of arriving at an answer to this question is to ask psychologists and sociologists how they define intimacy.

- Eric Berne is succinct in his definition: "Intimacy is a game-free relationship."[1]
- Keith Miller expands on this idea with comments from the book *The Single Experience*: "In an intimate relationship one feels safe to reveal hopes, dreams, fears, the past—including one's sins and mistakes. These things can be shared without the fear of being judged, condemned, or straightened out."[2]
- In his book *The Road Less Traveled*, Scott Peck tells us that intimacy is "the will to extend one's self for the purpose of nurturing one's own or another's spiritual growth."[3]
- Keith Miller continues his definition: "Intimacy happens when two people walk into each other's imaginations, each actually penetrating the secret places of each other's hearts and minds."[4]

When you and I hear these words, our hearts say, "Yes, I'd like to experience these things in my life." This inner desire suggests a common bond between people: deep inside, each one of us wants to be heard and wants to be known.

The Bible offers us further insight as to why we desire intimacy. Consider first what Genesis 1:27 teaches: "So God

22

created man in his own image, in the image of God he created him; male and female he created them." We see here that we are made in the image of God—and I believe that our intense desire for intimacy comes from our being made in His image. The intimacy of a relationship without hiding places is the model that God gave us all—single or married—so that we can understand how we relate to Him, to ourselves, and to others.[5] (See John 1:12, Matthew 12:50, and Romans 8:15-16 for further discussion of the intimate relationship that God wants to have with us.)

We can also see this call to various kinds of intimacy as God's call to us to be "functioners." Let me explain. I define "functioner" as someone who lives fully according to the purpose for which he or she was created. These people function completely. They are whole. They experience fullness of life. Functioners, therefore, are also fully alive when it comes to being intimate.

These functioners—as well as those of us who may not apply the label to ourselves—can all learn something by looking at the model we are designed to follow. To be specific, I find it interesting to consider that God is a relational God. The doctrine of the Trinity—that the three Persons of the Father, the Son, and the Holy Spirit exist as one God—tells us that God has been in relationship for all eternity. Our God—our Creator—is a relational God. It is no wonder that we find a sense of completeness when we enter relationships. We have not been created to experience wholeness in complete isolation.

We need, therefore, to start our journey toward intimacy with the realization that *God created us to be intimate*. Why do we need to say that? We need to believe that since God intended us to be in relationship and since He created us to be that way, then He also must have given us the capacity to become intimate. Let me repeat that. *Since God has intended and created us to be intimate, then He has also given us the capacity to be intimate.* I believe that the very hope we have for intimacy indicates our capacity to experience intimacy.

Nevertheless, I am tempted to stop and say, "Hey, it's not possible!" I still want to build that fortress and throw prayers over the wall. I still hear myself saying, "I am too frustrated with this. Intimacy doesn't seem to be something that I can achieve, so I'll settle for something less." My fear keeps me from accepting the truth that I do have the capacity for intimacy.

This capacity for intimacy is evident in two fundamental needs which are within each of us: the need to belong and the need for significance. A close look at each of these basic needs will help us understand the way we were made and why we live with such a longing for closeness.

The Need to Belong

This need should not surprise us in light of the biblical understanding we now have of God being relational and of us being created in his image. We all want to be in relationship to other people; we all want to belong. Such belonging implies community, and community is more than a group or a program. Community touches our desire to know and to be known.

It was during my childhood that I learned something of my own desire to be known. I remember a time when secrets were very important to me. My identity was becoming more clearly defined as I gathered secrets and recognized that I had my own secrets— that I had something that was me and only me. As I think back, I find it significant that I did not want to keep all my secrets. I wanted to find someone with whom I could share some of my secrets. I wanted a sense of belonging: I wanted the bond that came with sharing myself and being known.

Validating my experience (an experience we have all had), Erich Fromm says that one of a person's greatest needs

24

is to overcome isolation. In the words of John Donne, "No man is an island." You and I don't need their statements to realize the truth of what they are saying. It *is* important to belong.

Belonging, however, is frightening for at least two reasons. First, we realize that giving up a secret costs something: we must let ourselves be vulnerable. There is the momentary joy of sharing a secret. Someone else knows me! There is a bond, and I belong! That joy, though, is closely followed by the haunting thought, "Will he give my secret away?" Even when we are young children, that dread is very real. We have all followed a secret with the query, "Cross your heart and hope to die?" This vulnerability which accompanies sharing brings tension. Am I still safe? Will I be hurt because I shared? Although our desire to belong is intense, we are well aware that the stakes are high.

Second, belonging is frightening when we receive as well as share secrets. We find joy when our companion not only accepts our secrets but also reveals his or her own secret places of the soul. Initially, we experience the exhilaration that comes with knowing another person. We find this feeling soon followed, though, by a certain dread: "Can I handle these secrets with appropriate care?"

Still, the bonding that happens when we take the risk of sharing our secrets does provide for us a sense of belonging. We respond by talking about "my group," "my church," or "my club." Very often we seek this bonding in places where there is minimal threat, and that threat can come from two directions. In the same way that we fear being disappointed by our confidant, we are also afraid that we may be the one to disappoint the person who confided in us. Our need for belonging—for being connected to other people—is a need that can force us to risk, to trust, and to be intimate with another person in spite of our fears.

The Need for Significance

When I die, I want it said that Terry mattered. In other words, I want it to be important to someone that I lived. I want someone to feel that there was a reason for my time here. A story comes to mind . . .

One day, while jogging near a desert retreat house, I was ready to pass by a small boy who had just been dropped off by a school bus. He needed to walk up the same road that I was running on, so he shouted, "Can I run with you?" I motioned him to come along, slowed my pace appropriately, and introduced myself to my new running mate. His name was Stephen.

Stephen was in third grade and was quick to tell me several details about his life in general and about his day in particular. It wasn't long before he handed me a 4″ x 6″ card he was carrying. "Here," he said, "Look what I have!"

The card declared that Stephen had been named "Math Whiz" of his school, and he was beaming from ear to ear as I looked at the award. "Wow!" I said to him. "I'm impressed. You must really be good at math!"

He sheepishly replied, "Yeah, I guess so." Then without a pause, he said with certainty, "My dad is going to be *real* proud!"

There is something of Stephen in all of us. There is the hunger and the desire for someone in our life to be "real proud" of us. We realize as we grow older, though, that we can't be sure about the response of the people around us. We can't be sure that anyone will be proud, but still we try. Cautiously, we show a few people who are close to us our own "merit cards," all the time hoping that they will respond, "Wow! I'm impressed!" If their response is neutral, we are quick to explain, "Oh well, it wasn't all that important anyway"—but the lack of affirmation cuts deeply.

In contrast, it is interesting to note that we derive our greatest pleasure from the affirmation of people with whom we already feel we belong—from family, friends, or "our group." By the same token, it is with these people that we are most cautious when we have merit cards to share—"What if they don't think I'm significant? *Then* where would I turn?" This fear is tied to the fact that we are taught that significance is awarded on the basis of *what we do*, and not on the basis of *who we are*—a critical distinction that we will look at more closely in the next chapter. If what we have done is rejected or judged unimportant, we translate that as a rejection of our person and we begin to question our very self-worth.

Belonging and significance—these needs are common to all of us. As they provide us pictures of our souls, we see both our desire and our capacity for intimacy. We see both the joy that comes with affirmation and the fear of failure and rejection.

What, then, is intimacy? It is the place where we come to terms with our created potential. It is the place where we are free to acknowledge and express our basic needs to belong and to be significant. It is the place where we can be honest with the fears and doubts that plague us. It is that place of warmth that encourages and enables us to slowly let down our barriers. It is that place where we can share and where we can listen. It is that place where God becomes very real through His gift to us of another person.

The personage is that "me" which I wear or become in order to get people to accept me.

CHAPTER FOUR

Obstacles to Intimacy

The questions he asked were based on years of both frustration and hope. "Will I ever be able to let someone love me? Will I ever be able to love a person without wanting to change her? Will I always be stuck here?"

Which one of us has not, at one time or another, felt those same emotions and asked those very questions? Each one of us has felt stuck in relationships we know to be unhealthy and yet have found ourselves unable to move away from them. Often we fear leaving the familiar even though we want desperately to initiate a new relationship. Often we don't move because we aren't able to believe that intimacy is possible in our lives. We feel trapped by our fears and our questions—How did we get to this point? Where does this "stuck" feeling come from? Can we move from here? Where do we begin to change? Is intimacy even possible?

These questions call for the same kind of analysis as my work as a consultant for churches does. As a consultant, I am responsible for providing objective observation and for pointing out any obstacles that are preventing growth. In this chapter, I will provide a consultation on the topic of intimacy. Together we'll look at this feeling of being stuck and then I'll suggest some obstacles which may be blocking your path to intimacy.

Our difficulty begins with our inability to look at truth. To be honest, truth frightens me. Why? Because truth dispels illusions. And when I am stuck, it's usually because I remain committed to illusions. Truth, though, allows me to see myself as I really am and therefore gives me the freedom to move on—and that movement into the unknown can be scary.

In his book *The Meaning of Persons*, Dr. Paul Tournier offers some important insights on this subject of identity—this subject of seeing who we are—by pointing out that there are really two persons in all of us. One he calls a *person*; the other he calls a *personage*.[1]

Person

Our *person* is the natural expression of who we are. It is my true self—the real Terry Hershey who exists beneath all of my defenses and masks. We see this true self (or person) most clearly in young children. Their emotions and reactions are natural outpourings and therefore accurate reflections of what is within. Like children, our persons do not second-guess or anticipate. There is no caution in expression, and therefore it is real, it is authentic, and it is current.

In an adult, that person is difficult to find. It remains buried—partially, if not entirely—under the behaviors which allowed us to become socially acceptable and "normal." (Let me add that in our culture it seems more important to be normal than to be real!) Furthermore, as we examine this subject, we will see that "probably everybody has a more or less concealed inner chamber that he hides even from himself and in which the props of his childhood drama are to be found."[2] It is there—in these secret chambers—that our person resides.

Personage

In defining this term from the vantage point of a practicing physician and psychologist, Dr. Paul Tournier writes, "I become increasingly aware that the person, pure and unvarnished, will always escape us. Doubtless only God knows it. I can never grasp the true reality, of myself or of anybody else, but only an image; a fragmentary and deformed image, an appearance: the personage."[3]

Having been introduced to these terms, consider now how each one of us is an interesting mix of person and personage. It is our inability to understand this mix that creates obstacles to our personal growth and to our growth in relationships.

First, where do these personages come from? Let's look at an example from Tournier's book—an incident which takes me back to my own childhood. Let's call the boy in our example "Willie." Although Willie is only four, his parents have taken him to church. At one point during the service, Willie decides that his coloring book is not very interesting. He begins to fidget and look around the church. It so happens that the minister has reached a point in his sermon that requires the special emphasis of pauses and whispers. It also happens that right in the middle of one such pause, Willie turns to his father and says, "Daddy, who's that man up there talking?"

Tournier finishes his eye-witness account: "Doubtless it is the first time he has been brought to church. He has not been trained in the social conventions yet. His father is very embarrassed, and instead of answering his quite natural question whispers to him to be quiet. But around me I catch one or two smiles, as if the child's spontaneity had in some way brought a welcome relief, as if a window had been opened, and fresh air allowed to blow where the weight of solemnity was beginning to be rather stifling."[4]

We must remember that what is at stake here is not the social or moral rightness or wrongness of the father's response. More important than what is right or wrong is that which occurs in the heart and mind of Willie. He doesn't know quite what to think of his father's command to be quiet. Father even looked angry, and Willie isn't sure why. In order to satisfy his own curiosity, Willie tries the same question the next week. Only this time, he asks his mother instead. His mother responds by glaring at him and pinching his leg, hoping to quiet him. What is Willie supposed to think about his parents' reactions? What will he learn from their sharp commands and stern looks?

Just like you and me, Willie's behaviors will be shaped by his desire to be accepted, to belong, and to be significant. Not yet understanding social protocol, Willie can only interpret his parents' reactions as rejection. He is learning that he will be awarded and accepted on the basis of what he does. It appears to him that his behavior must change—or, in other words, that he must be something other than he is—in order for his parents to accept him. He is not confident that he will be accepted simply for who he is.

Unbeknownst to Willie, but very apparent to us, Willie is learning that a personage is often necessary if he is to elicit a positive response from significant people in his life. "Don't they like me the way I am?" becomes an issue for all of us at one time or another in our development.

Consequently, in order to experience the acceptance and belonging that he so desperately desires, Willie begins to discover—although not necessarily consciously—those personages or masks which elicit the desired responses from Mom and Dad. This process of discovery can go one of two directions.

If after church Willie's parents affirm their love for him and explain the reason they were embarrassed by his question, Willie may begin to understand the necessary social role that this "be-quiet-in-church personage" must play. He may then begin to give serious effort to playing the game of "being quiet in church" because he knows that Mom and Dad will be proud of him.

If, on the other hand, Willie's parents do not address his questions, Willie will be left to assume that he is a very bad boy for asking what he considered the very legitimate question, "Who is that man?" Unable to live with that conclusion and unaware that his parents would be proud of his quiet behavior, Willie pursues the only method he knows to insure that he gets Mom's and Dad's attention: his ill-timed questions become a regular occurrence in church. His parents' response to him is never warm, but at least he gets them to respond.

We see Willie, very early in life, learning what all of us have learned: in order to receive the acceptance and belonging we desire, it may be necessary to wear an appropriate personage or mask. We have learned, too, that there is a difference between our person and our personage. The personage is that "me" which I wear or become in order to get people to accept me. Why? Because I begin slowly cultivating the assumption that when and if I show them my *person*, it will be inappropriate and unacceptable. It therefore becomes easier for me to learn new personages.

In her book *The Drama of the Gifted Child*, Alice Miller captures this tension between person and personage. She vividly describes an individual coming to a significant realization about himself. The person—and each one of us—comes to understand:

> ... that all the love he has captured with so much effort and self-denial was not meant for him as he really was, that the admiration for his beauty and achievements was aimed at this beauty and these achievements, and not at the child himself. In analysis, the small and lonely child that is hidden behind his achievements

wakes up and asks: "What would have happened if I had appeared before you, bad, ugly, angry, jealous, lazy, dirty, smelly? Where would your love have been then? And I was all these things as well. Does this mean that it was not really me whom you loved, but only what I pretended to be? The well-behaved, reliable, empathic, understanding, and convenient child, who in fact was never a child at all? What became of my childhood? Have I not been cheated out of it? I can never return to it. I can never make up for it. From the beginning I have been a little adult. My abilities—were they simply misused?"[5]

As we look back on our own lives, our purpose is not to undo our childhood or to become bitter about a childhood that completely repressed our person. Our purpose is not to blame but to understand: such an understanding can be a stepping stone toward freedom.

Also, we can see that our wish to understand our present relationships, our desire to build healthy relationships, and our need to find belonging and significance must be preceded by our recognition of the very real tension between our person and personage. If we do not understand, we are destined to remain stuck. We will continue in our futile attempt to find belonging and significance through a personage, and we will continue to believe the myth that people like us because of what we do rather than because of who we are. Once we acknowledge and begin to understand the difference between our person and personage, we are free to continue our journey toward intimacy.

The most comfortable way for us to be sure of another person's approval is to cater to whatever we think that person wants to see and hear.

CHAPTER FIVE

Where Do Our Masks Lead?

His question was sincere, but I knew that I couldn't give him the answer he wanted. He was a successful man in his late forties with a winsome personality that enhanced his good looks. Relationships were not the issue for Tom. He had plenty of relationships. His problem was finding one that would last. He had a history of relationships which lasted for one or two years and occasionally for only a few months.

"I don't know what I'm doing wrong," he said. "Do you think that there is anyone out there who will love me as I am?"

I wanted to say yes, but that wouldn't have helped Tom. Tom's problem lay in his inability to see the difference between his personage and his person. In his own words, he gave people what he thought they wanted, and then he wondered why he always ended up empty.

Tom seemed stuck. He seemed firmly rooted in a behavioral cycle which didn't allow honesty or openness. It was a cycle that didn't allow him to reveal his person. This behavioral cycle—not an uncommon one—is the direct outcome of a misunderstanding of our person and personage. We will refer to the cycle as our relational-behavioral cycle, and it looks like this:

1. Dependence Stage

I base my identity on your approval or rejection of me. I believe that I'm loved for what I do, not for who I am.

4. Interdependence Stage

At this first step toward freedom, I finally realize my ability to peel back a corner of my mask and share my person.

2. Independence Stage

I attempt to retain a sense of self-worth by isolating myself. I want to avoid being rejected.

3. Slavery/Oppression Stage

I become a victim of my need to have other people make me okay.

1. Dependence

According to what we learn about our personages, we begin to respond to those around us with appropriate behavior: I repeat behaviors for which I am rewarded and I stop behaviors for which I am punished. Or, as I mentioned earlier, if I am in a relationship where punishment is the only source of attention I receive, I continue with my wrong behaviors in order to receive attention (i.e., punishment) from you. Either way, I am at the stage of dependence.

At this point of dependence, I sacrifice—or at least repress—my *person* so that I will receive your approval of my *personages*. How many of us have grown up slaves to the comment, "What will people think?" "What they think" becomes the determining factor in our behavior. In the words of Alice Miller, "There are still many situations where he [Dr. Miller's patient specifically, but any person in general] sees himself as other people see him, constantly asking himself what impression he is making, and how he ought to be reacting or what feelings he ought to have."[1]

I could recount a number of stories about people—both men and women—who are angry and hurt about the failure of their marriages. As they talk with me in my office, a frequent and heartbreaking comment is "I married him/her because my parents wanted me to!" The variations on that theme have no end: "I became a minister because my mother wanted me to" or "I had a child because my parents needed a grandchild."

Dependence creates an environment where wrong or unhealthy choices are a natural consequence. Why? Because I need your approval, and I make decisions according to what I think will win me that approval. I am dependent on your positive reaction to me, to my words, to my actions in order to feel good about myself. Tournier describes people in this state as no longer being men, "but merely puppets worked by some anonymous stage manager pulling the strings behind the scenes."[2]

Without realizing it, we have bought into a myth which says, "If I show you my person, you probably will not like it or accept it. Therefore, I'll play it safe and give you a mask I know you'll like." The truth is, of course, that we don't really know what another person's response to us will be. But because of our strong need for acceptance and belonging, we seek the path of least resistance to our goal: the most comfortable way for us to be sure of another person's approval is to cater to whatever we think that person wants to see and hear. Using a mask or personage seems an easy way to gain a sense of belonging.

This observation leads us to an important relational principle: Because of the discomfort and tension caused by my desire for acceptance and my fear of rejection, I make comfort the essential criterion in relationships. The comfort

comes when you accept me—or when you accept the personage that I show you.

What is the result of this mentality? I don't enter a relationship out of concern or affection for you. Instead, I
approach you and take you hostage! You are something of a
prisoner because I need you to make me okay. If it appears
that my person will not get me the acceptance and belonging
I desire, then I will wear the appropriate mask(s). You, in
turn, will find me acceptable.

This dependence that I've described is not always the
result of a conscious decision on our part. From childhood,
we develop "personage programs." Our programs consist of
those series of masks we wear at appropriate times for the
appropriate people. The game we play involves knowing
when to switch the masks. A friend of mine puts it this way:
"So intently do we practice who we think we are that we
prefer the act to being who we really are."[3]

When we are at this stage of dependence, our energy is
consumed by our urgent need to find the appropriate mask
and by the fear that the one we choose will not be the right
one. In the dependence stage, then, we slowly come to build
a false self. No longer relying on our real emotions, we find
ourselves slowly becoming alienated from ourselves as well
as from those around us. As this alienation takes place, we
move to Stage #2.

2. Independence

So confused are we by the conflict between our natural
emotions and those personages we feel we must adopt in
order to be accepted that our true identity is threatened.
Though as children we may not ask the question "Who am
I?," we are nevertheless very much aware of the fact that we
function best in an environment of nurture and acceptance.
When our natural behaviors do not elicit these reactions, we

experience an identity crisis as we wonder why we haven't been accepted.

How do we respond to this? We look for some place where our real emotions, our inner secrets, and our deepest fears can be safe. That place is isolation or independence. At this point we make the important realization that our own secrets are significant. It is as if we can now say, "My secrets are important." Still, our fear of rejection remains with us even after we move from the state of dependence. This fear drives us inside ourselves, and we become a fortress for our personal secrets.

When our parents ask such simple questions as "Did you go to school with Billy today?," we find ourselves lying—not because we want to lie, but because we have a strong desire to protect our secrets. We think to ourselves, "This information is something that is *mine*. Something that my mother doesn't know. Something that is *me*."

This move toward independence is an attempt to establish an identity in spite of a fear of dependence—and this is no small step. The fear of dependence is basically the fear of rejection: I am afraid of being dependent on you because I am afraid of being owned by you. You would own me because I would find myself in the situation where everything I do is dictated by my fear that you will reject me.

But sooner or later, my understanding of my identity becomes clouded. I become unsure of which voice—your voice of approval or the voice of my person—is reliable and which will be my master. The result is movement to Stage #3.

3. Slavery/Oppression

Any choice I make will have certain consequences, and these consequences will automatically confine me by determining any future choice I might make. Once I decide to jump off a building, for example, I am no longer free to jump. I am a prisoner of that choice to jump and of whatever consequences that action may have. Likewise, once I put on a certain personage or mask, I must act according to that mask. I am no longer free to be myself. Instead, I am a victim of the choice I made to don that mask, and I am a slave of whatever consequences that choice now presents to me.

Interestingly, this slavery can come from a choice of dependence or from a choice of independence. As we saw at Stage #1, my tendency to act in ways that will win me approval can come to tyrannize my life. Ironically, my independence at Stage #2 can also become a dependence of sorts. When I make the choice to hide, to build walls, and to isolate myself, I become dependent on, or enslaved by, that choice. Having therefore entered Stage #3 from either the point of dependence or independence, I have taken yet another step away from my person. At this point of slavery to my personages and my earlier choices, my life will be characterized by the following:

a) My energy is focused on polishing my personages.

I have become addicted to someone around me for affection and a sense of belonging. As a result, I am concerned more than ever before about what others are thinking and saying about me. I am convinced that a person's acceptance of me is based solely upon the masks I wear. Maintaining these masks requires time and energy, and I find myself drained.

Ironically, when all of my energy goes into maintaining my personage—that thing which wins me affection—I find that there is no energy remaining for the relationship itself. Furthermore, I begin to believe that my personage is the total definition of who I am, and the result is that there is no time for me to be who I really am. I am enslaved to my personage, and therefore . . .

b) I put myself into relationships which confirm that personage.

44

When my choice of a relationship encourages a personage rather than my person, I am living out a self-fulfilling prophecy. I expect acceptance only of my personage. That personage, then, is all that I share in our relationship and that relationship serves to confirm my prophecy: you accept this personage so you certainly wouldn't accept my person. An example will illustrate how this way of thinking works.

Consider both the woman who chooses the mask of "men love me only because I'm a plaything" and feels expendable in the relationship and the man who chooses "women love me only because I'm tough." When the love or acceptance stops, these two people will be hurt and angry. They will also be blaming: "See! I told you they wouldn't like me!" In all likelihood this man and this woman never shared anything of themselves: they had entered a relationship wearing the mask of plaything or toughness (a *personage*) and then regarded the eventual end of the relationship as a confirmation that they (their *person*) could not be accepted. Having set themselves up for a fall, they nevertheless blame the person who rejected them. Furthermore, they let the end of that relationship confirm the personage—the mask—they were hiding behind.

This kind of hiding can be even more confining as I become addicted to my need to have you accept me. This need forces me to perform for you. Then, having become dependent on you or addicted to your approval, I am unable to see who I really am. I cannot see myself apart from my personages or from the person whose acceptance I value.

People who find themselves at the place I have been describing will often play the victim: "Because I am dependent on you for acceptance, I will allow myself to become the victim in our relationship. I will not stand up for myself; I will not express opinions, frustrations, or hurts. After all, I am probably not good enough to deserve your love anyway. I will therefore tolerate whatever treatment you give me as long as you show some degree of acceptance."

45

c) Being enslaved to my personages and this need for acceptance, I repress my real emotions and feelings.

Once I have assumed that you will accept only the appropriate personage, my real feelings go underground. If I tell you what I am really thinking, you may not approve of me or accept me. When I repress my feelings like this, though, it's as if I am trying to hold a large beach ball under water. The fact is, of course, that both my hands will be occupied holding the beach ball down. In the same way, when we repress our true feelings, most of our energy is spent holding down those feelings.

Consider what happens when the beach ball is eventually released. Does it float gently to the surface? No! In fact, due to the easing of the pressure required to hold it under, the ball shoots out of the water in an unpredictable and unexpected direction. In the same way, I find my repressed emotions coming out in unpredictable ways or in unexpected and inappropriate places. Repressed anger, for instance, easily becomes resentment or bitterness. Repressed worry becomes anxiety. Repressed jealousy becomes hatred. Repressed hurt can become resentment or self-hatred. Consider now this example of repression.

Bob and Judy had dated for almost two years, but I was not surprised when they came to me for counseling.

"How's your relationship going?" I began.

"Just great!" Judy jumped in immediately. "In fact, we just wanted to spend some time with you so that you can confirm what we already know. We're good for each other and we would like to get married."

"Okay, I'll help where I can. Let's start with you both telling me how you resolved your last fight."

Again Judy jumped in: "Oh, we don't fight. We get along in everything. And we agree on everything we do."

"If that's true," I replied, "then (a) one of you isn't necessary and (b) you don't need me."

They both stared at me with blank expressions. I turned to Bob. "Does it bother you that Judy answered both my questions and didn't give you a chance to reply?"

Again Judy jumped in. "No! Bob likes it that way."

"Then let's ask Bob," I said.

Bob glanced quickly to Judy and then began, "It's okay, Pastor. She always talks first. I don't mind."

Before he finished, Judy interrupted again. "That's not true, Bob. If you'd only show a little more assertiveness, I wouldn't have to do all of the talking."

From that point on, the conversation—as might have been expected—became explosive. Both Judy and Bob had been repressing their real emotions for months, maybe even years. The emotions which had shown themselves in subtle, hurtful ways were now out in the open. The outburst revealed how both Judy and Bob had become slaves to personages that did not fight or disagree.

In Stage #3, then, our person and personage(s) grow farther apart. We will, for instance, do or say something only to think immediately afterwards, "Wait a minute! That's not really me!" Obviously, just like Stages #1 and #2, Stage #3 will make us victims of our unhealthy behavior. It is important, first, to realize that we ourselves choose to become victims and then to remember that no one can force us to choose anything. Consider whether you might be in Stage #1, #2, or #3, and then read the next chapter. It can help you choose to free yourself from whatever personage is tyrannizing you.

47

Interdependence is the freedom to choose to tell another person who I really am.

CHAPTER SIX

Interdependence:
A Move Toward Freedom

I learned recently of a certain tribe in Africa that has a unique way of catching monkeys. These people first collect coconuts which are too heavy for a monkey to carry, and then they carve a hole into each coconut. After emptying out the milk, they put food into the shells and lay them out so that the monkeys will find them. When a hungry monkey approaches a coconut, it reaches in for the food. The hole, however, is too small for the monkey to pull out its fist. If it lets go of the food, it could very easily get its hand out of the coconut. Instead, rather than letting go of that precious bite of food, the monkey will allow a person to pick it up and carry it away.

This story was interesting to me because it reminded me of us. We humans are a lot like that monkey. We, too, tend to clutch trinkets of life even if it means losing our freedom to move on. We sacrifice the chance to live abundantly as we cling to things which only seem important. These trinkets are the personages behind which we hide. In this chapter on interdependence, though, I want to challenge you first to let go of whatever trinket—whatever dependence or personage—you are clutching and then to peel back a corner of your mask. You will begin to experience the freedom of

51

interdependence, a freedom which breaks the cycle of dependence, independence, and oppression.

As we've seen in the past two chapters, maintaining this cycle slowly takes its toll on our relationships. Sooner or later, we find ourselves settling for that which we know to be unhealthy. We lower our expectations and live within the confines of our dependencies. This pattern is, of course, nothing new to the human race. We find an example of this cycle occurring as far back as history is recorded. In Genesis 3, we find an account of the first relational problem. Let me set the scene.

As we saw earlier in the book, human beings were created to be in relationship with God and with each other. (See Genesis 1:26-31, 2:15-18, and 2:23-25.) Human beings were also created free—free to express their *person*, free to express emotions, free to express needs and desires, and free to express hopes and fears. God never intended for us to be slaves or victims: His plan for us is freedom. What happens in Genesis 3, however, sabotages this freedom and begins to destroy relationships.

Take time to read Genesis 3:1-13. Here man takes total responsibility for his identity—for his person. Consider that act and its consequences. Having disobeyed God and eaten the fruit from the tree in the middle of the garden, Adam and Eve did in fact gain wisdom as the serpent had promised. Acting on this wisdom, the man and woman sewed fig leaves together in order to cover their nakedness. That project completed, the two of them heard "the sound of the Lord God as he was walking in the garden" (verse 8)—and they hid from Him.

Having earlier eaten the fruit and thereby assumed total responsibility for their identity, their immediate reaction now is to protect what they have. Not confident that this protection is sufficient, they become afraid and they hide from God. Why? *Because they assumed that God would not accept their person, naked and vulnerable.* So what did they do? They made a personage—in the form of leaves—and hid.

Centuries later, we still respond just like Adam and Eve did: we create a personage to protect ourselves and then we spend much of our energy sewing new leaves. Our relational-behavioral cycle is a trap of dependence, independence, and finally oppression. Consequently, we relate to one another out of our needs to *hide* and to *hurl*.[1] First we'll look at the need to hide.

Look again at Genesis 3:10. When God calls out to Adam, he answers, "I heard you in the garden, and I was afraid because I was naked; so I hid." Similarly, when we try to find our worth by looking just to ourselves, we become fearful. What happens if someone does not accept me as I am? Not wanting to deal with this possible rejection, I feel that I must hide.

When I hide, I am saying that I want to be perfect, that I want to belong, and that I want to be significant. I know, though, that I am not perfect, and I feel that I don't fully belong and that I'm not truly significant. I can't allow you to see these things, however, because then you would find me unacceptable. Therefore, I must hide from you. And how long will I hide? Until I am perfect.

In our culture, this kind of hiding has become a very sophisticated art. We hide in a variety of ways—some of them quite noble. Hiding is noble, for instance, when we are busy working for the Lord. While this appearance may gain us a certain respect from people, the fact remains that we *are* hiding. Other people find hiding places behind busy schedules, excessive eating, speaking in religious cliches, drug and alcohol dependence, nervous giggling, and gallows laughter. Ironically, whenever I hide and whatever I hide behind, I am still acting out of my dependence on you: my fear that you will reject me compels me to project the personage I hope you will accept.

53

In this state of dependence, I find that my relationships are characterized not only by *hiding*, but also by my need to *hurl* at you as well. Look at the words and blame hurled in Genesis 3:12-13. When God asks Adam and Eve whether they have eaten from the forbidden tree, much finger-pointing takes place:

> The man said, "The woman you put here with me—she gave me some fruit from the tree, and I ate it."
> Then the Lord God said to the woman, "What is this you have done?"
> The woman said, "The serpent deceived me, and I ate."

Adam responds to God with his classic excuse: "God, I've been meaning to talk to You about the woman You gave me!" Adam does not want to take responsibility for his disobedience. He wants to escape the charge of any wrongdoing and thereby be free to feel okay about himself. Likewise, in my state of dependency on you, I want to feel okay about myself. Consequently, I place a lot of pressure on you to make me okay. When you do not respond the way I'd like, I choose to hurl blame at you.

When I hurl, I am saying that I want you to be perfect. After all, I need you to make me okay. You must provide me with a sense of belonging and significance. But you're not perfect, and I make matters worse by projecting my own imperfections and insecurities onto you. I become angry that you aren't able to make me okay. What I'm actually angry about, though, is my own incompleteness. When will I quit this blaming and hurling? When you become perfect. As long as you aren't perfect and therefore don't make me okay, I will hurl at you.

As with hiding, we are quite sophisticated in our blaming and hurling. We have, for instance, perfected the art of gossip, often thinly disguising it as a prayer request—"Yes, let's pray for her. But please fill me in on all of the details, so that I can pray intelligently!" We also find ourselves offering mockery, excessive criticism, and judgment of another person or situation. This hurling can affect important relationships with people close to us. It's easy to see, for example, that in approaching my relationship to you with a strategy of hide and hurl, I set us up for failure. This course of action, though, accurately reflects my own insecurities: I am afraid to succeed with you. If you accept me as I am—for no apparent reason—I can't understand it. I will not be able to justify your love for me.

Am I to be forever confined to this hurtful game-playing? Must all of my relationships be characterized by hiding and hurling? Is there hope for me if my life up to this point has been spent polishing my personages? Besides, am I to assume that all personages are evil? That if only I could rid myself of them then my person would appear and I could lead a life of complete honesty? Even Tournier contends that my hope of finding my unadulterated person by stripping off all personages is an illusion.[2] What, then, comes of someone who feels stuck in this stage of slavery and dependence? There is a step that each of us can take, and that is a step towards interdependence.

4. Interdependence

Interdependence means a life of honesty about our person—about who we are. Interdependence involves peeling back one corner of my mask in order to reveal to myself and to someone else the person—not just a personage—who is there. Interdependence, therefore, is the doorway to intimacy. Interdependence does not deny the existence of personages. Neither does it condemn their existence or propose that we go through the remainder of our lives without any of them. In fact, in our ordered society, personages often play an important part in social protocol. (My person, for example, may want to hit you, but that action is not socially acceptable.)

What, then, is interdependence? *Interdependence is the freedom to see that my identity is not locked into my personages. Interdependence is the freedom to choose to tell another person who I really am.* Interdependence begins with honesty. It calls for both the willingness to be honest about my dependencies and the acknowledgment that I am not stuck with them forever.

We are not quick to move toward interdependence, though, because we assume that peeling back a mask means ripping off the entire thing. Ironically, we often attempt what we call intimacy by doing just that. We will go to someone and "dump" everything! We tear off what we hope is the entire mask. This dumping is *not* intimacy. It is *not* interdependence. It is still a sharing born out of fear and dependence. Dumping is not based on healthy sharing. Instead it is based on an "I dare you to like me" attitude: we often anticipate that the other person will not fully accept what we share, and our dumping turns that expectation into a self-fulfilling prophecy.

Needless to say, steps toward interdependence are not easy. We are, for instance, afraid to peel back a corner of a personage because then we can see negative emotions. We must come to understand, though, that our emotions are not negative in and of themselves. They are merely signals that allow us to see what is going on inside our person, and they may be telling us that they are hiding something which needs to be uncovered. Furthermore, we must come to understand that it is okay for us to be where we are—even though that may be a place of anxiety or fear. Only as we are able to acknowledge where we are can we move on. The acknowledgment may involve a simple statement: "Thank You, God, that I am experiencing anxiety and fear. These emotions tell me that I am going through the process of the person/personage struggle. They allow me to stop and work on that struggle."

Acknowledging emotions like this is an important step toward interdependence. As long as the emotions are mine—and they become mine when I acknowledge their existence—I can make a choice about dealing with them. If I realize that I am anxious about something, for example, I can change that feeling. I own that feeling and can deal with it. It is not your fault that I am anxious, and I am not merely waiting for you to do something to change my anxiety. I am not a victim who leases emotions from you at the very expensive rate of dependence, independence, or slavery. I am owning my emotions and can deal with them. Still, some of us continue to wish for magic. A secret chant or special potion would certainly be easier than facing what is inside of us.

Let me reassure you that we need not fear our emotions. They are signals of our person—they are indicators of what is going on beneath our various masks—and they can become our teachers and friends. If we are afraid of them, though, we will hide from them. We will continue to let our mask conceal what we are feeling. If we choose to freely share our emotions, however, we are free to be intimate first with ourselves and then with another person. Intimacy with self involves being open and honest about one's own ideas and feelings, and that's an important first step toward intimacy with another person. We don't need to fear our emotions: we can instead appreciate them as they nudge us toward interdependence.

Interdependence is difficult not only because it can involve fear of our own emotions, but also because it involves risk. Most people, therefore, approach relational encounters with a lot of hidden defenses. I know that I often come armed! I have knives, guns, and brass knuckles to protect my person. Interdependence begins, though, only when there is unilateral disarmament: it begins only when I take the risk of peeling back a mask, of removing a personage. With this risk, I begin to set myself free. I will no longer let myself be a victim of what you think about me. I will no longer let myself be enslaved or paralyzed by fear of your rejection. Instead I will be free to make my own choices. I will be free to move forward. I come to understand that intimacy can be a reality. I realize that I can share myself if I am willing to pay the price of overcoming fear and taking some risks.

As you enter the stage of interdependence, the rewards will far outweigh the cost. You will finally realize your ability to peel back your masks. You will realize your ability to share your person. Interdependence will enable you to experience fuller and richer relationships. Interdependence, for instance, allows you to give and to love because you no longer have to be a victim. Interdependence also allows you to receive because you don't need to be completely isolated from relationships in order to protect your identity. Interdependence enables you to respond, not merely react, to people and events. If you are to experience wholeness or failure, then it will not be because you took a passive stance and waited for life to come to you. While choices to be dependent or independent lead only to slavery, the choice of interdependence leads to freedom—and freedom leads to life. Intimacy *is* possible, and interdependence allows it to happen.

When we hear God, we learn our true identity. When we hear God, we know our true master.

CHAPTER SEVEN

Who Owns Me?

A recent magazine advertisement caught my eye. Sponsored by a local humane society, it was promoting the purchase of pets from the city pound. The full-page ad featured a heart-tugging photo of a puppy and kitten which was introduced by the following phrase: "It's who owns them that makes them important." Besides being a very effective (not to mention cute) ad, the message touches a fundamental truth about people. *We derive our identity and significance from whoever or whatever owns us.*

Not long ago, Bob Dylan wrote a song entitled "You Gotta Serve Somebody." This simple title introduces a profound truth. In the song, Dylan says that whether we're rich or poor, a king or a pauper, famous or unknown, we all have to serve somebody. Let me add that we often serve that person or thing which offers us a sense of significance or belonging.

In response to the two basic needs to belong and to be significant, we search for the person, experience, or object which will meet those needs and provide us with the sense of acceptance and security that we so desire. We saw in chapter 5, though, the truth that dependence upon any person outside of ourselves to meet those basic needs leads ultimately to oppression and slavery. Where, then, do we go?

How can we find freedom from slavery to another person's possible rejection of us? How can any of us answer the gnawing question, "Who am I?"—a question which ultimately is "To whom do I belong?"

Let me set forth a reality that is undeniable. If we have not yet come to terms with the question of our identity—the question of who owns us—then we will inevitably struggle with relationships, personal fulfillment, sexual ethics, and any other issue which touches our life. Not one of us wants such a struggle. Instead, we hope and dream for a future which includes peace about ourselves, freedom from our past, and confidence to move ahead. Those dreams are not unreachable possibilities reserved only for the "super-spiritual." On the contrary, the Bible is clear that God created us to enjoy the fullness of life. He created us to enjoy peace, freedom, fulfillment, and joy. (See Matthew 10:29-31, John 10:10, 2 Corinthians 5:17, and Jeremiah 17:8.)

Can we come to know the fullness of our dreams? If God's Word is true, the answer is a resounding YES. We are not destined to mediocrity or discontentment. To begin to fully realize our dreams of an abundant life, though, we must again face the truth that "It's who owns us that makes us important"—it's who or what owns us that gives us an identity and gives us significance.

Let's begin with a look at the way in which we come to understand our identity. Think of each of us being born with an imaginary piece of paper deep inside. This paper is our Identity Checklist. On that checklist goes the variety of things, persons, and events which give us some kind of answer to the question, "Who am I?" Many of us have never stopped to examine that checklist. We may therefore be surprised to discover what things have found their way to our checklist—we may be surprised to see what is defining who we are. Many things try to tell us who we are.[1]

- Our *society* and *culture* tell us that we are a number. Consider how your name becomes almost insignificant in the midst of a social security number, a driver's license number, credit card numbers, phone numbers, checking account numbers—the list goes on and on. Furthermore, we use numbers against each other as we continually rate, evaluate, and judge one another on, for example, a scale of 1 to 10. All the while, we fantasize about moving up the scale, and we support our fantasy by joining health clubs, using the right makeup, and wearing designer jeans. We are honest enough to admit that we are not 10s. In fact, we are probably 6s. But we sure wouldn't mind dating an 8 or a 9! We lose who we are and who other people are when a person is reduced to a number.

- Our *job* tells us that we are what we do. You are what your skills are. What if you are unemployed? Do you lose your identity? What if you believe your particular skill is inferior to another person's skill? Does that make you an inferior person? How often do we hear comments like, "I'm only a housewife" or "I'm only a factory worker"?

- Our *school system* tells us that we are a grade. You are what you produce. This pressure to produce doesn't encourage education or learning; instead it pushes people to attain that all-important grade. Once a grade is assigned, a person has an identity: "He's a 'C'-student" or "She's an 'A'-student."

- Our *parents* tell us who we are—regardless of our age. They tell us, for example, that we need to be what they couldn't be, and the pressure on us to perform for them can sometimes be relentless. Not long ago a fifty-two-year-old man confessed to me his fear of inadequacy. When I asked if he had any ideas about where this feeling came from, he replied, "My father always wanted me to become a lawyer like he was. But I couldn't cut it. And I've spent my life working construction. I feel like a failure."

"Have you talked to your father?" I asked.

"No," he said softly. "My father's been dead for fifteen years."

Even though his parents were gone, they still controlled this man's identity and he was unable to break free.

- Our *labels* for ourselves and for others tell us that we are a certain status, and in our culture, it is important to obtain the "right" status. Furthermore, we like labels because they help us categorize people. We can put them into mental boxes that are tagged "divorced," "never-married," "single," "charismatic," "fundamentalist," "Bible-believing," "born-again"—the list is endless. Once we've labeled a person, we feel that we know who he or she is and we can deal with him or her.

- Our *marriages* tell us who we are. At times we feel as if we are merely an extension of our spouse. I may be known only as so-and-so's husband. She may only be known as someone's wife.

- Our *churches* tell us who we are. They tell us that we are Christians or that we are "spiritual" by what we wear, by what we say, by what we do, or, ironically, by what we don't do. I was taught, for instance, that "we don't drink, we don't chew, and we don't go with girls that do." This illustration is extreme, but the message is that we must fit a certain mold to be accepted as "Christian" or "spiritual." The church accepts us, once again, on the basis of our performance.

- Our *sins* tell us who we are. All too aware of our failings, we feel unlovable. We struggle with guilt. We also contend with Satan, the father of lies, who tells us that we are worthless. Again, performance is the key issue—and we feel that we'll never be able to measure up. If we feel the need to try, we tend to want to pull ourselves up by our bootstraps—and that approach misses the whole theology of grace.

With all of this data on our Identity Checklist, its' easy to see how the result can be an unstable identity. It is no wonder that we are easy prey to the dependence-oppression cycle we looked at in chapter 5. Let's look at how this unstable identity develops and how we can deal with it.

First we choose an identity package and become a slave to it. Just like Adam and Eve, we are afraid of our nakedness and vulnerability. Desperately searching for appropriate leaves to cover us, we put together our identity package. We begin by collecting items or personages for our Identity Checklist, always hoping to find that place where we can feel comfortable being us. Advertisements for these identity packages sound very familiar:

- "You only go around once in life. Grab for all the gusto you can!"
- "If only I could accumulate enough to be comfortable, I would then be able to enjoy life."
- "With the right use of my talent, I could really be successful."
- "With the right amount of power, I could control my life."
- "If only I were a 10, people would accept me for who I am."
- "He enjoys life—and I would, too, if I had his money."
- "Because I've been divorced, I am destined to be a failure in relationships."

There is a time when we give ourselves wholeheartedly to the pursuit of our identity package. Inside, we hope desperately that this package will bring us the belonging and significance we desire. It doesn't take us long to realize, though, that our efforts end in disappointment: we have been pursuing an illusion. We have learned the hard way that our pursuits lead not to freedom, but to slavery.

In truth, we can never do enough to complete our Identity Checklist and feel content about who we are. I can never do enough to be a "10": I can never feel secure about my identity if on my own I am trying to define and mold that identity. With each rung of the ladder, I become only more painfully aware of the fact that there's always another rung above me. Besides, even if I were to arrive, my greatest fears would be losing what I've obtained and being unable to find peace in my achievements.

One consequence of this pursuit of both my identity and a degree of perfection or fulfillment is the development of a certain type of legalism in my life. Since my continual focus is upon my need to make the mark (whether that mark be earning straight "A's," working at a prestigious job, or getting a raise), I find myself continually defining and redefining the line of achievement. With the hope that one more accomplishment will give me significance, I continue to push myself towards a goal in order to attain acceptance and approval. In reality, however, no number of achievements or successfully reached goals will complete me.

At this point, let me clarify something. The desire to achieve is not wrong. Furthermore, we shouldn't stop setting goals for personal growth. Neither should we feel hopeless about reaching those goals. I am claiming, though, that our identities and our goals need a firm foundation. We must listen to Jesus' parable about the men who built the house (Luke 6:46-49). One built his house upon sand, the other upon firm ground. When we are a slave to an identity package, we are building a house of achievements on sand. The accomplishments may look good, but they will soon fall and they will constantly need rebuilding. The issue here is our foundation: it's who own us that provides us that foundation.

Our identity will be unstable, though, when we base it on our achievements—an act which results in our living with a spirit of discontent. When we are enslaved by this elusive identity package, we can never be satisfied with who we are. Always faced with another rung to climb, we become discontent people. We are not thankful for who we are or what we have. This spirit tends to become resentment of God: "God, you sure didn't deal me a fair hand in this life!"

Being so driven to perform, we find our spirit further characterized by anxiety, and we often experience great letdowns after significant achievements. We read, for example, of many Olympic athletes who have won gold medals and yet have not been happy: they arrive at the final step of defining their identity package only to realize it is not enough. Consider, too, the professional dancer whose feelings of significance are dependent on his ability to perform. When that dancing ability is lost, so is his identity. Identities built on performance or accomplishments are indeed houses built on sand.

Although as slaves to an identity package we may find ourselves feeling discontent, we may nevertheless remain right there in our comfort zone. We *know* that comfort zone: being miserable is familiar to us and we can nurture the illusion that we are still in control. Moving away, even from unhappiness, involves taking risks and facing some unknowns.

Having looked at various sources of identity and at some less than healthy consequences of those sources, now it is time for the step of acknowledgment. What are you chasing to make you feel adequate, loved, significant, and whole? What are you enslaved by which gives you a sense of identity? Who or what owns you? These questions are difficult ones. Where do we begin to find answers? Where do we turn for freedom? Are we destined to this enslavement for our lifetime? Is there hope?

Earlier in this book, we affirmed the fact that God desires us to be whole and fully alive. We must not forget that fact. And it is important to remind ourselves of this as we feel ourselves pulled in various directions by many different owners or masters. Listen to the New Testament promises and encouragement below:

- "It is for freedom that Christ has set us free. Stand firm, then, and do not let yourselves be burdened again by a yoke of slavery."—Galatians 5:1
- "Don't let the world around you squeeze you into its own mould, but let God re-make you so that your whole attitude of mind is changed."—Romans 12:2 (Phillips)

Each of us needs a solid foundation as we come to know ourselves. Eugene Peterson is helpful here when he reminds us that a Christian's real problem is not in attempting to achieve freedom, but in "learning service under a better master."[2] We need to come under new management. Let me suggest steps toward doing this.

1. We can acknowledge our present situation.

Whether we like it or not, all of us are owned by someone or something, and we need to acknowledge this fact. We have given the control of, or the authority over, our identity to someone or something. Our master (that to whom or to which we have given control) then tells us who we are, what our values will be, the types of relationships we will have, and the direction of our future.

What do our masters look like? They come in a variety of shapes and sizes. For some, a master is another person or a relationship. We are owned by—and consequently dependent upon—that person to define who we are. For others, a material object or the need for many possessions can be a master. Still others are enslaved by the need to be loved, the need to achieve, or the need to be "successful."

How do we begin to deal with this situation? The Bible calls us to confession, and this confession begins with an acknowledgment of our present condition. Until we tell God where we are, we are destined to stay there.

All of us, however, want to move on without confronting where we are. It's difficult and it can be quite painful to look at ourselves and to honestly evaluate our situation. Such an

evaluation means, for one, taking responsibility for ourselves. Instead, many of us want to be guaranteed a rosy
future without taking responsibility for today. Simply put,
confession is taking such responsibility. It is recognizing that
we need to feel significant and that our tendency is to sell
ourselves to any master that promises this significance.

The Bible calls this tendency our sin nature: it is my
attempt to do things *my* way. Confession, however, says this:
"God, I know that You are my Creator. I know that You
continue to dream a dream for my fulfillment. I confess my
desire to give my life to masters other than You. I have been
looking for significance in the wrong places. Thank You for
offering me genuine significance and a stable foundation for
my identity in Your love for me."

Consider for a moment who or what owns you. To whom
have you given your identity? What is it that you seek on your
merry-go-round for significance? Answer these questions for
yourself as I have had to do for myself. You and I can move on
only as we stop and look at who we are and where we are
now. We can move on only as we are honest. We can move on
only as we acknowledge and confess.

2. We can be willing to hear God and be changed.

In John 5, we hear Jesus asking what might be considered a
very insensitive question when He says to a man crippled for
thirty-eight years, "Do you want to get well?" I believe that
instead of being at all insensitive Jesus is touching a fundamental reality about that man—and about each one of us.
And that reality is that *the presence of pain does not guarantee a desire for healing.* Change is difficult because change is
painful, and change is painful because it calls for responsibility. Change asks that we give up our present master and
move on. The initial step of confession and acknowledgment
now calls for the willingness to change. This step can be

scary when we have grown comfortable in our state of discontent.

Consider now another story from the gospel of John. In chapter 21, Jesus talks with Peter for the first time since Peter had denied knowing Jesus a few days earlier. It's interesting to note the focus of Jesus' concern. He asks Peter, "Do you love me?" Let me paraphrase that simple question this way: "Peter, will you accept your relationship with Me? Do you acknowledge your present condition? Do you hear My words for you? Peter, you can feed My sheep. Your identity is free from other masters—free from your failure, your past, your guilt, your need to repay, your need to impress, and your need to be right."

With the question, "Do you love me?," Peter is asked to hear God, to allow God to tell him who he is, and to allow God to own him. Like Peter, when we hear God, we learn our true identity. When we hear God, we know our true master. When we hear God, we hear the call to be free from those things which tyrannize us by their oppressive mastery.

And we hear God when He speaks to us through the Bible, His Word. In it, He says some powerful things about our identities:

a. God says that we were created in His image. (Genesis 1:27; Psalm 8:4-5)

I can and should see myself as a personal creation of the Creator's loving hand, and this perspective should completely alter my identity package. With loving care, God formed each one of us as an undeniably unique person, each with exquisite details which give us an identity unlike any other creature.

b. I am potentially related to God. (John 1:12)

Because of this gift of new life in Jesus Christ, I am given the opportunity, the privilege, and the authority to call God my Father. Here, I find that my identity is no longer tied to what I have done or to what I have failed to do. Instead, my identity is tied to a gift freely given, and that gift is God's love.

In essence, accepting God's love is what it means to become a Christian. Until I receive this gift, I am stuck as a "god-player": I assume responsibility for giving meaning to my existence and for running my life. But we have seen that playing God like this leads to slavery because we can never do enough to be whole.

Becoming a Christian, then, means receiving God's gift of His Son, Jesus Christ, who lived, died, and was resurrected for us. Becoming a Christian means being redeemed—or being bought back from the life of slavery to self. When we become Christians, God takes our identity packages and in return gives us a new life in which we are free from the need to perform. Becoming a Christian is learning service under a better master, and all this can happen despite our complete inability to earn God's love.

If you have not received the gift and become a Christian, the offer is available now. I invite you to receive God's gift of love. You can pray this prayer: "God, I've wanted to be in control. I've spent my life playing God. I've been wrong in these actions and I'm tired of where they lead me. I acknowledge and confess to You my prideful ways. Thank You for Your Son, Jesus. Thank You for Your gift of new life. I receive it."

c. The Creator has given us, as His children, value and worth. (1 Peter 1:18-19)

When I receive God's gift of love, then I can see that my identity no longer needs to be tied to that which is around me. Ultimately, all of those masters to which I had sold my identity will die, or rust, or pass away and leave me empty.

But God's gift of His love never fails: it remains constant when all else is unstable and it will last through eternity.

d. I have the capacity to accept whatever state I'm in. (Philippians 4:11-13; Psalm 40:1-2)

I can accept whatever situation I'm facing because I am living in God's love. I am no longer a victim of externals or of the circumstances of life. These circumstances no longer determine my identity, so I can accept them. I can stand confident in God's love for me. I have realized that I do not need someone or somewhere or something else for joy to be mine. I don't need to gain status or gather belongings for wholeness to be mine. My journey toward wholeness begins when I receive God's love.

Confession, the step by which we first acknowledge our present master and then turn to Jesus Christ, allows Him to become the new master: Jesus Christ will be our Lord. We will find ourselves under His management. Still, change can and probably will be difficult. All of us want weight loss without sweat. We want vitamins without spinach. We want the peace that God gives without letting Him be our Master and without giving up the master who now owns us.

3. Having heard God's word, we can choose to live as if what God says is true.

It is not easy either to acknowledge our present condition or to hear what God says about us. A major reason for this difficulty is the fact that we are caught between conflicting ideas. We want to believe that we are precious, yet we are driven by our need to earn love. We want to believe that God loves us, yet we continue to base our worth on what we do and on whom we know. We want to believe that God gives us significance, yet we seem convinced that we can never do enough to be okay. Like Adam and Eve, we are unable to

72

believe that God can accept us naked and vulnerable, and therefore we spend energy sewing fig leaves together. We have a hard time believing the truth of God's grace and of His amazing love for us.

What, then, is our next step? We make a choice: we choose to live "as if." Let me give you an example from my childhood. . . .

My friends and I would often fish with a spear—a pastime requiring patience and skill. It was not long, though, before I learned an important lesson. If I threw the spear at the fish, I always missed by twelve to eighteen inches. Why? Because the water gave me a distorted perspective of depth. In order to hit the fish, I actually had to throw the spear above the fish. In order to become a good spear fisherman, I had to learn not to trust the perspective of the water. If I did, I knew I would miss the fish. Instead, I needed to throw the spear twelve to eighteen inches above the fish I wanted to get, and I had to act *as if* that fish were truly there.

This lesson I learned as a boy illustrates our struggle with our identity. *We can live based upon the input of the thing or person which currently owns us, or we can hear what God says about us and live as if that were true.* Let me ask you some questions: If you believed that you are valuable because God said so and if you acted *as if* it were true, would your life be different? If you believed that God's love for you is not based on your performance and if you acted *as if* it were true, would your life be different?

Obviously, the answer to both questions is yes. The issue, of course, is *how*—how do we act *as if*? The answer is found in John 21 when Jesus says to Peter, "Follow me!" Like Peter, we act *as if* by hearing and doing. By hearing and doing. By hearing and doing. In other words, we can't live the Christian life until we live the Christian life. Think of the $10 bill you have in your pocket. It is worthless until it is used—until you put it in the bank or spend it. You can talk about the $10 bill all you want, but it is only yours when you use it. Likewise, on

73

paper—on the pages of the Bible—we belong to God. That fact makes no difference in our lives, though, until we use it. As we try to use it—as we try to live *as if*—we will be battling the Enemy (Satan) as he tries to defeat anything that God wants to do. The battle of ignoring the Enemy and the voices of the world and instead hearing the voice of God is not won overnight. The battle of who owns me—the battle of my identity—is fought daily.

The good news—should we hear it—proclaims that we are free from the oppression, the tyranny, and the rule of other masters. The good news is that we can choose to hear the voice of a new Master (John 10). The good news is that it is He who owns us who gives us significance. And in that light we are significant indeed!

We talk about God; we talk at God; we talk to God—but seldom do we talk with God.

CHAPTER EIGHT

Intimacy With God

"She came to see me at the recommendation of a friend. She had been troubled for years, seeing psychiatrists seriatim and not getting any better. The consultation had been arranged on the telephone so that when she walked into my study it was a first meeting. Her opening statement was, 'Well, I guess you want to know all about my sex life—that's what they always want to know.' I answered, 'If that is what you want to talk about I'll listen. What I would really be interested in finding out about, though, is your prayer life.'

She didn't think I was serious, but I was. I was interested in the details of her prayer life for the same reason that her psychiatrists had been interested in the details of her sex life—to find out how she handled intimate relationships."[1]

In relating this experience, Eugene Peterson touches on a fundamental and painful truth: we are never so vulnerable as when we talk with God. Such vulnerability is reflected in our behavior: we talk *about* God; we talk *at* God; we talk *to* God—but seldom do we talk *with* God. Certain emotions that we tend to associate with God and prayer—emotions such as guilt, confusion, apathy, and anger—further underscore our vulnerability by touching raw nerves. This touch reminds us that we are not whole in and of ourselves.

"Intimacy with God?" The young woman seemed surprised by my use of this phrase. Her response suggested that, for her, the words "intimacy" and "God" were definitely incompatible in the same sentence.

I repeated my question: "Have you ever desired intimacy with God?" She had come to me with a history of relational failures, each one of which reinforced her already low sense of self-worth.

After some silence she responded, "I guess I've never thought about intimacy with God."

"You long to be known and loved by a personal God," I commented in a somewhat questioning tone.

"Yes, certainly" was her immediate reply.

"And that longing makes sense," I said, "for we were created to find such fulfillment in relationship with God. To understand life abundant is to understand a life where one is known and loved without the fear of being straightened out."

"That's not possible for me," she objected.

"Why is that?" I asked.

"Because if God really knew me, I don't see how He could love me."

Vulnerability. The fear of being known. The fear of being loved. The fear of being rejected. In the past few chapters, we've seen how these fears both affect and infect our identity as well as our relationships. Our fears cripple and even immobilize us.

I believe that these fears are rooted in a more basic fear: our fear of God. How we come to understand that fear and how we deal with it will directly determine our sense of self-worth and, in turn, our freedom in human relationships.

As we begin to think about the issue of intimacy with God, I want to review some points from the previous chapter. That discussion of identity was built on two assumptions. I claimed, first, that everybody is looking for life—for wholeness, completeness, peace, and fulfillment and, second, that it is who owns you that gives you your source of life. If those assumptions are true, then there is no such thing as an atheist. Everybody has a god. The gods may take on different shapes and sizes, but everybody has a god. And each of us seeks from that god a sense of purpose and fulfillment. We seek from that god a sense of belonging and significance. This is what I am referring to when I speak about intimacy with God. And all of us—religious and nonreligious—need a source of identity and significance. Our ability to find intimacy either with our own god or with God Himself will then determine our ability to find intimacy with each other.

Christianity—the choice of God over various man-made gods—is unique because the God of Christianity is a personal God. Christianity offers intimacy with the God of the Bible, the God of creation, the God of history. Furthermore, the God of Christianity is a God who seeks us out. He wants to be intimate with us, and He pushes us to be known. In the face of this God who wants to be in close relationship with us comes the fear of vulnerability we will talk about next.

Where does this fear originate? I believe that we get a glimpse of our answer in Genesis 3, a passage we saw earlier as pointing out man's tendency to *hide* and *hurl*. Both of these obstacles to intimacy with others are rooted in our inability to find intimacy with God. Genesis 3 paints for us this picture of man's vulnerability, his fear, and his consequent need to hide even from—or maybe especially from—his Creator.

Genesis 3 comes after the Genesis 1 and 2 account of the creation of the world and of us human beings. These chapters teach us, among other things, that we were created with the capacity to receive significance and fulfillment from our Creator. It was and is the desire of our Creator that we enjoy to the fullest the life He gave us. *Being created* implies the very fact that we are receivers of life. Purpose, significance, and fulfillment all come to us as a gift from God.

What happens in Genesis 3, however, is a fundamental shift in the way in which we approach life. We move from being receivers to being takers. When God created us to receive, He said, in effect, "Trust me. I will provide for you."

Our response tends to be this: "That sounds good—but that means we must rely upon You as our source of life. Wouldn't it be easier if we took on that responsibility?" And isn't that exactly the temptation put to Adam and Eve when the serpent said to the woman, "You will not surely die . . . for God knows that when you eat of it [the fruit] your eyes will be opened, and you will be like God, knowing good and evil" (Genesis 3:4,5).

This temptation—one which each of us faces daily—is the temptation to take control of our own destiny. In taking control, we also take full responsibility for our own identities and full responsibility for finding a source of significance and fulfillment. And if that is my responsibility, then I can no longer afford to be a receiver. I must instead become a taker and see to it that my identity is carefully defined and maintained.

As a taker, then, I approach life from a defensive and protective stance: if I am responsible for my identity, I can ill afford to lose anything I have gained! I fear losing what I have taken in my attempt to manage my life and establish my identity. I therefore find myself very vulnerable in the presence of anyone who might come to know me, and so I hide. As a taker, I feel the need to protect this vulnerability. After all, if I were known by another person, how could I maintain control of my life?

Approaching life as a taker—as one in charge of establishing my own identity—also affects my relationship with God. As a taker, I do not let myself receive from God, and I no longer see God as the giver of life. Instead, God becomes my enemy: I fear His ability to see through my protective charade. This distorted picture of God is worth looking at closely because as long as we misunderstand God, we are doomed to misunderstand love and intimacy. Once our picture of God is reworked, though, we can find healing for the hurts we've experienced. We can see God from a new perspective and we can achieve a new kind of intimacy with Him. First, however, we need to acknowledge where we are now. When we realize how our approach to life as takers affects our behavior, we'll then be free to move forward.

1. First, our perspective as takers requires us to relate to God on a performance basis.

As takers, we seem convinced that our worth comes from that which we take, that which we earn, that which we perform, or that which we deserve. So convinced are we that our worth is based on what we do, that God's offer of unconditional love is, at best, remote and, at worst, unimaginable. As takers, we can only see love in terms of accumulated points. We feel what one man expressed succinctly and emotionally at one of my seminars: "No one would love me for no reason!"

With this statement, the speaker has touched the heart of the human being as taker. Any worth apart from that which is earned, that which "makes sense," or that which meets conditions is difficult to understand and accept both emotionally and intellectually. It is no wonder, then, that we become hiders and hurlers. Other people become competition and conquests, and God becomes the Judge who, waiting in the wings of the stage of life, stands ready to flash the scorecard which will destine us either to eternal doom or eternal joy.

How does intimacy with God fit into this mind-set? Not easily! This pressure to perform (a self-imposed pressure, I might add) shifts our focus from God to ourselves and therefore affects the way we relate to God: rather than being the giver of life, God is now Someone from whom I must earn or for whom I must perform in order to enjoy His acceptance and my own worth and significance. If intimacy with God seems out of reach, it is no wonder. Ironically and sadly, many of our churches have perpetuated the idea that we must perform for God's acceptance, and this distorted idea leads to the second.

2. Thinking that God loves us according to our performance encourages us to become dedicated to the practice of religion.

Religion is basically a human structure: it is our attempt to understand and experience intimacy with God. Religions, though, tend to be built on the human assumption that self-worth comes via performance. Let me offer an example from my own life.

As I grew up, holiness or spirituality became something I *did*, not something I *was*. I remember as a child getting the distinct impression from several sermons that when we toe the line, God will be proud of us. Therefore I, like many, gritted my teeth and toed the line. "We don't smoke, and we don't chew, and we don't go with girls who do!" became our ethic of behavior. Sure, the rules were clear and I was following them closely—but was I experiencing fullness of life? No, I was practicing religion.

Another way in which a mere practice of religion manifests itself is in one's prayers. Prayer, for instance, can too easily be reduced to a formula I recite or a ritual I perform in order to earn points from God. Rhetoric and cliches can replace sincere prayer. Also, prayer to a presence that reminds me of my vulnerability may even become something that I avoid at all costs. Either way, it is no wonder that the idea of intimacy with God seems foreign and unattainable!

A religion that is so performance oriented is another attempt to remain in control of my life. It is my way of maintaining full responsibility for my own identity, but only now I've spiritualized it. One unfortunate side effect of my confinement in this "religion" is my need to apply my own perspective of life—that self-worth comes from performance—on everyone around me. Consequently, I become judgmental and very concerned that others toe the line—*my* line—as well. This notion that God rewards us for our performance has resulted in a rather warped practice of religion, and this view of religion can lead very quickly to an even more debilitating and confining understanding of God.

3. Performing for God leads me to see God as a dispenser of trinkets of significance.

Although I am feeling that I need to perform in order to win God's acceptance, I am at the same time tempted to hold God responsible for performing for me. Many well-meaning Christian people view God in this light, and I believe that this perspective has its roots in our "taker" mentality and in our inability to understand true intimacy with God.

I have, for instance, heard many people say that their level of faith allows them, as children of the King, to petition God and even to demand a certain performance from Him. The unspoken words behind this tell me that "level of faith" is a spiritual way of talking about a right I have earned (there's that word again!) which allows me the opportunity to treat God as the Grand Provider who is obligated to grant my wishes. A closely related but more subtle teaching is the message that if we only had more faith, we would experience fewer troubles. In both instances, the word "faith" is used euphemistically for the idea of performance: God will make me somebody if I have enough faith (i.e., if I perform well enough).

The theme that has run through these myths about our relationship with God is becoming increasingly clear: fear and performance; performance and fear. We fear our nakedness and our vulnerability. As takers, though, we feel obliged to cover up and protect our own nakedness, and so we perform. We sew fig leaves together in an attempt to hide. The more we perform and hide, the more afraid we become

83

of being found out, of being left naked, and of being out of control of our lives. Much of our religious activity and therefore much of our relational activity becomes centered on the sewing together of fig leaves. We continually create new and ingenious ways to cover up our fundamental fear of being naked—a nakedness which reveals our human need to receive. When the motivation in a relationship is this kind of fear rather than love, it is extremely difficult to be intimate!

4. As takers and performers, we become easy prey for the demon of destructive self-fulfilling prophecy.

A taker assumes full responsibility for his/her identity, for his/her life, and consequently for his/her destruction as well. Let me explain. So fearful am I of my nakedness that my life becomes one continual pursuit of that encounter, that person, or that possession which will give me significance. I work diligently on perfecting my performance in the hopes that one day it will command a standing ovation from those around me. All the while, though, I am aware that fig leaves are never permanent. I am therefore never fully comfortable with their covering. In response to my own intense fear of being known and of my drivenness to keep that from happening, I find myself controlled by a new variation of performance—martyrdom. I find significance in being used, beaten, dumped on, mistreated, or put down. I find my significance in letting you walk on me.

My martyrdom can come in another way as well. Afraid that I am unable to accumulate the proper points for God's affections, I devise a new way to get His attention. I do this by making certain choices and decisions. I choose friends, for example, who reinforce my fear and my sense of inadequacy. Consider Sally's story.

Sally was a lady in her thirties. She was attractive and pleasant to be around. But Sally seemed haunted by a demon of self-destruction. When she came to see me, she was in the process of being rejected by the eighth man in three years. "Am I all *that* bad?" Sally wanted to know.

Instead of answering her question, I tried another approach. "Why do you want to fail?"

"What? I *want* to fail?" She went on. "I guess I've never believed that I deserve God's love."

I finished her thought: "And so you sought to prove that you were right. And you have succeeded. You've gotten into relationships where you set yourself up for failure. You have sabotaged them from the start, and when they ended, you were able to say—even with some distorted sense of pride and accomplishment—'See! I told you God didn't love me! I told you I wasn't worth His love!'"

Sally is not unique in this behavior; she is not alone with this demon. It is common to many of us, and it robs us of life and of wholeness. Lest you think I am getting a bit over-dramatic by using the word "demon," let me explain. My purpose is not to conjure up any thoughts of *The Exorcist* or of demon possession. I see demons, though, as anything that the Enemy (Satan) uses to take away the life that God created us to enjoy. And a self-destructive spirit does just that: it robs us of God's gift of life abundant.

Having considered the path away from intimacy with God—a path characterized by pressure to perform—let's now look at how to stay on the path toward Him. We can enjoy intimacy with God. Hear these words of King David—words which offer us hope:

> O Lord, you have searched me
> and you know me.
> You know when I sit and when I rise;
> you perceive my thoughts from afar.
> You discern my going out and my lying down;
> you are familiar with all my ways.
> Before a word is on my tongue
> you know it completely, O Lord . . .

Where can I go from your Spirit?
>Where can I flee from your presence?
If I go up to the heavens, you are there;
>if I make my bed in the depths, you are there . . .

For you created my inmost being;
>you knit me together in my mother's womb.
I praise you because I am fearfully and wonderfully
made;
>your words are wonderful,
>I know that full well . . .
How precious to me are your thoughts, O God!
>How vast is the sum of them!
Were I to count them,
>they would outnumber the grains of sand.
When I awake,
>I am still with you . . .

Search me, O God, and know my heart;
>test me and know my anxious thoughts.
See if there is any offensive way in me,
>and lead me in the way everlasting.
>>*(Psalm 139:1-4, 7-8, 13-14, 17-18,23-24)*

David is a man who understood intimacy with God. Able to face both his own vulnerability and his need for control of his life, he was also able to find release and freedom in God's love. What can we learn from David?

• We are called to a lifestyle of confession.

Unfortunately, the word "confession" has received much bad press. We tend to think of confession primarily as a recitation of our faults. Confession, however, is much more than that. Consider Psalm 139. David reveals his understanding that he needed to rethink his life. He needed to evaluate who

86

really is in control. This same thought process—this act of confession—leads to a change in one's perspective on life. It can lead to a change in our understanding of control just as it did for David.

Simply put, confession is my willingness to say, "I am not God. And I don't even wish to apply for the job! Furthermore, I am incomplete. I am not all that He created me to be, and He can do a better job of helping me become that person than I can do on my own. Perhaps now I'm finally in a position where I can understand what it means to receive life as a gift from God." Confession is a willingness to let God be God. Like David, we can come to see God as the God who seeks us out and who desires us to experience intimacy and completeness.

This point is worth repeating: God desires intimacy with us. Our misconceptions about a God who responds to us only on the basis of our performance crumble under the power and beauty of the Christian message that God so desires intimacy with us that He has initiated that relationship. In John 14:26, God confirms His intention to share an intimate relationship with us when He sends His Holy Spirit to us. The Holy Spirit is God's Spirit. He has a personality. He has a role as the one who draws alongside us. He guides, comforts, protects, and prays for us. His presence reminds us of God's presence: the Holy Spirit is God's message to us that He is committed to a relationship with us.

Confession, therefore, is not merely a recitation of faults. It is not brow-beating ourselves before the Creator of the universe. It is not wallowing in our failure. Instead, confession is sharing ourselves. It is openly sharing our inadequacies with God. David understood this when he wrote Psalm 139. He shared his inadequacies—his sins—and came to a new understanding of this God who desires to intimately know and be known by His people.

Henri Nouwen supports this concept of confession when he writes about the role of prayer in an intimate relationship with God: "Prayer creates that openness where God can give himself to man. This openness . . . requires our confession that we are limited, dependent, weak and even sinful. Whenever you pray, you profess that you are not God and that you wouldn't want to be, that you haven't reached your goal yet, and that you never will reach it in this life, that you must constantly stretch out your hands and wait again for the gift which gives new life . . . it makes you vulnerable."[2]

As Nouwen's words and the prayer that preceded it suggest, confession changes a person's focus. Confession is the acknowledgment of where I am that first allows me to take responsibility for my past and for my present and then allows me to give that responsibility and control back to the proper owner, God Himself. I thereby acknowledge that I can be set free to move on. I am no longer confined to my need to be in control.

If I am still viewing life with a sharp focus on my performance, though, confession is very difficult because then I see God as judging me and my worth on the basis of my confession. The result is more guilt for my inability to measure up. I find myself afraid to confess and unable to give control back to God for fear that He will not like my confession. I convince myself then that *after* I "get my act together," I'll give control back to God.

In a lifestyle of confession, however, we come to see our incompleteness not as a cruel trick from God or as a threat to our own enjoyment of life, but as a necessary requirement if we are to approach life as receivers. When we see our emptiness in light of His fullness, we can more freely receive all that He wants to give us.

- **We are called to give responsibility for our identity back to God.**

As I've said, I approach life as a taker when I see myself as solely responsible for my identity and my wholeness, and it doesn't take long for that responsibility to become an oppressive tyrant. I can never do enough to be whole. I can never sew together enough fig leaves to protect my identity. I can never accumulate enough relationships to provide me with a sense of worth and significance. Life lived as a taker, therefore, is life in a continual pressure cooker.

In Psalm 139, David offers us the good news that the pressure can be lifted. He had learned that his identity is intact in the hands of a loving and faithful God. In those hands, I—like David—am set free from my need to perform, from my need to control, and from my need to take. I no longer need to feel responsible for everything that goes on around me. I no longer need to feel responsible for what others think, for what others do, for the way circumstances unfold, or for my own sense of self-worth. I will no longer have to perform for God or show Him how strong or how good I am. I will no longer need to fear my nakedness. My vulnerability will no longer be an enemy. Instead, that vulnerability can teach me to receive from God.

When I let God be God, I will be set free. I will come to realize that God's love for me is not based on how religious I have been, on how well I perform, on how much I have accumulated, or on whom I know. I will see that God's love for me is freely given. It is my responsibility to respond to that love. It is my choice to become a *receiver* of His love. In receiving, I am saying, "I acknowledge God as God, as the source of life, the source of love, and therefore the source of my identity. I acknowledge the temptation to perform and to take in order that I might overcome my weakness and incompleteness. I realize that my performance has not given me freedom or fullness of life. I return that responsibility to God."

Learn from David and his picture of God. Realize that God seeks to be intimate with us. He seeks to know us and be known by us. He wants to redeem us, to enfold us, to give Himself fully to us. His gift of life is brought to focus in Jesus. We need only to open ourselves to receive His love.

One wise person has observed that rules break, but people tear. What we want to avoid is tearing other people (and ourselves) in our expressions of our sexuality.

CHAPTER NINE

Slaves in a Free World

As Cathy spoke, it was evident that she was trying to cover up a sense of hurt and confusion. Involved in a relationship where there was a high degree of sexual involvement, Cathy was realizing, deep down inside, her discomfort with the relationship. Basically, the relationship was an unhealthy environment for her growth as a person.

"What's interesting," she observed with a sense of frustration, "is that I do not really even enjoy sex."

"Why, then, do you find yourself so sexually active with this man?" I asked.

"I want to be held," she responded, and the tears began to fall. "And that is the only way I know to get him to do that."

Sex, in many ways, remains a mystery to all of us. It evokes such emotions as confusion, excitement, guilt, anger, and hurt. How, then, can we come to understand our sexuality?

The "sexual revolution" of the '60s and early '70s promised freedom and "free love." While it is true that, in the words of a 1983 *Psychology Today* article, "we have been liberated from the taboos of the past," we now "find ourselves imprisoned in a 'freedom' that brings us no closer to our real nature or needs."[1]

93

The world in which we live bombards us with sex. Mel White describes the barrage of "... billboards, magazine ads, television programs and commercials, behavior manuals, plays, films, books, magazines, popular music, bumper stickers, jokes, clothing styles, display windows, posters, even printed T-shirts (THIS BODY IS MINE, BUT I SHARE) ... At the heart of this sexual overload is the popular lie that sex is an answer for our larger human needs and pressures."[2] Ours is a world where we seek from sex, for instance, a guaranteed fulfillment of our emotional and even spiritual longings. Sex is projected as the answer—as "a kind of glorified patent medicine for everything that might ail us."[3] Ironically, though, notes one student of our modern culture, "today there are men and women who can talk about their most intimate sexual behavior as if they are describing a stroll in the park, then become flustered and embarrassed at the mention of love."[4] Obviously, we have strayed far from a healthy perspective of our sexuality as being a gift from God. Society, though, cannot be blamed completely for our skewed attitude about sex.

Consider, for instance, how our tendency to approach life as a taker affects our way of thinking about sex. When we need to take from other people in order to establish our own identity, sex becomes merely another dispenser of significance for us. We buy into the implicit promise that sex will provide us instant intimacy, better self-esteem, stronger emotional ties, a more solid commitment, and a confident sense of self-worth—all of this via performance, of course!

I believe that our difficulty with and confusion about our sexuality lie, too, in the basic difficulty we have with intimacy. I believe that because we do not understand intimacy, sex becomes distorted, confusing, and even ugly. Unfortunately, society feeds that distortion: we are bombarded by sex, we tell jokes about it, we blush in its presence, but few of us have come to terms with it.

Into this world alive with sexual stimuli and implicit promises of freedom, we take our already unstable identity structures, and then we wonder why our relationships—rather than encouraging intimacy—become obstacles to the intimacy we seek. Along with our unstable identities, we bring with us "the baggage of the past, our internalized cultural limits and weaknesses. Thus freedom—in this case sexual freedom—increases choice, but it guarantees nothing, delivers nothing."[5]

Our desire in this chapter is not to dwell on what may already be evident about our sexuality and what our culture teaches us about it. Neither are we interested in creating a theory about sexuality or establishing a set of definitive rules for sexual behavior. Instead, it is my hope that we can be set free—free from our confusion about our sexuality, free from myths we've learned along the way, free from our fears of inadequacy, free from the failures of our past, and free from being stuck in negative lifestyles. It is my hope that we can gain an understanding of what we are as sexual beings, of how that informs our capacity and longing for intimacy, of "what we tend to make of ourselves, and of what we can be through grace"—through God's grace.[6]

As we begin this process, I am aware of two immediate emotional responses: excitement and caution or fear. On the one hand, I find that the very mention of sex can arouse me. I can become easily stimulated by a conversation about sex. I am not sure, though, what to do about this sense of excitement for it is accompanied by a sense of guilt that suggests that my excitement is inappropriate. Still, recognizing these feelings is important. Only as I acknowledge the presence of the excitement (and any guilt or other feelings) can I deal honestly with the issue of my sexuality.

A second emotional response to conversation about sexuality is fear—the fear of being discovered. Consider the awareness of our vulnerability that comes with just the mere mention of our sexuality. As Adam and Eve covered themselves to protect their very identity, they covered their emotional, psychological, and spiritual nakedness as well as their physical nakedness.

It is easy to understand something of what Adam and Eve must have felt. Each of us well knows how closely our sexuality touches our identity. Our sexuality, therefore, is a point of great vulnerability. We fear being discovered and we fear being rejected. When there is talk about sexuality, I sometimes feel as if it is uncovering my very soul. I am uncomfortable. I am afraid.

Where *do* these powerful emotions come from? And are they normal? We can misunderstand such emotional responses if we do not understand the relationship between our sexuality and our personal growth. First, we experience vulnerability because our sexuality is very much a part of our personhood. While our tendency has been to separate our sexuality from our person, reality tells us that we do not simply carry a body around. Reality tells us that we *are* a body. We were created by God as sexual beings. It is precisely because we are created as sexual beings that the outworking of our sexuality is not an inconsequential matter.

What we do as sexual beings has definite consequences on who we become as persons. We cannot separate our bodies (or our sexuality) from our personhood. Donald Nicholl is helpful here: "For what we do with our bodies, what we put into them, how we treat them, what use we make of them, these are spiritual tasks which we are called to carry out in the name of holiness. There is no division in reality between the material and the spiritual: our spirituality is manifested by our treatment of matter."[7] If what Nicholl says is true, then it is possible and even essential that my sexual experience be integrated into my journey toward intimacy.

An inadequate understanding of myself as a "body person" leads to one of two unhealthy views of reality, either of which affects our ability to be intimate. Actually, this entire discussion dates back at least to the time of Plato. He argued that there were two worlds—a physical world and a spiritual world—and that that which belongs to the spiritual world is good while that which belongs to the physical world is evil. Our body—and hence our sexuality—is part of the physical world. According to Plato, then, our sexuality is evil, and this view exists even into our times. We still separate the body and the spirit, and if the spirit is good, the body must be evil. The outcome of this way of thinking is unfortunate and unhealthy.

We may, for instance, see the body as sinful. We may be raised on the notion that if it feels good, it is wrong, The extension of this view is that sex is merely a necessary evil— necessary only for the propagation of the human race. Sex is not to be enjoyed and is certainly not to be part of our journey toward intimacy and wholeness. Many well-meaning married men become mechanical in their sexual behavior for this reason. After all, sex is not to be enjoyed, is it? Our idea that our body is evil won't let us enjoy sex. It will also cause us to spend most of our energy pretending that we have no sexual desires.

Another possible result of the Platonic world view is the idea that our body is inconsequential. The tension between, on the one hand, the sexual urges and desires I feel and, on the other hand, my uncertainty about how appropriate or spiritual these feelings are can be intense. I can avoid this tension and freely enter sexual activity merely by treating my body—however consciously or unconsciously—as unimportant. A comment made by a prostitute reveals this very attitude. When talking about her work, she said, "That's not *me* in the room—it's just my body."

This prostitute and many other people as well adopt the viewpoint that their body is not important. They hope thereby to avoid the tension between their sexual urges and their uncertainty about how to deal with them. As they try to separate themselves from their body, they let themselves believe that they are no longer as vulnerable or as responsible in their sexual relationships. This unhealthy thinking that one's body is evil or unimportant will be an obstacle as we try to build healthy relationships. We will tend to keep our sexuality in check, we will pretend that it doesn't exist, or we will completely ignore the issue of responsibility with the thought, "Whatever happens, happens!"

We must, however, learn to see our sexuality—our sexual desires and our capacity for sexual enjoyment—as normal. They are a part of God's creation—a creation that He pronounced "good" (Genesis 1). We must see our sexuality—our capacity to touch and to hug, our capacity to admire another person—as a *gift* from God. I appreciate C. S. Lewis's reminder that "pleasure is God's invention, not the devil's."[8]

When I understand that my sexuality is natural and normal, I save a lot of energy that would otherwise be used either for repression ("Sex is bad") or for pretending that my sexuality doesn't matter ("It's only my body"). These attitudes, though, are harmful as well as inaccurate. You *do* have a body that was created by God and therefore is good, and your body *does* matter. God created us to understand these things about ourselves and to enjoy fullness of life. His Son echoed that when He said, "I have come that they may have life, and have it to the full" (John 10:10). Since Jesus desires that we be fully alive, it can not be His desire that our sexuality be an obstacle to wholeness or intimacy, to belonging or significance.

Again, I don't believe that this desire is an accident. Instead, I see it as reflection of our created purpose: we were created to enjoy fullness of life. We were created to find fulfillment in intimacy. We were created to function as whole beings. We were created to be *pro-life*. In order to remove the term "pro-life" from just the issue of abortion, think of it as coming from the phrase "pro(mote)-life." Now the term can apply to all ethical and emotional issues; now it emphasizes the importance of wholeness and completeness. Now the term "pro-life" is appropriate for a discussion of our sexuality.

If we were created to be pro-life—and I believe we were—then our relationships can be pro-life, our approach to sexuality can be pro-life, and our approach to life itself can be pro-life. Let me clarify what pro-life means in this context. Behaviors and attitudes are pro-life when they promote completeness, peace of mind, growth, joy, and health. In regards to sexuality, then, we want to become people who make choices that lead to health, not disease; to freedom, not bondage; to wholeness, not brokenness—in essence, to life, not to death.

In reality, however, we are aware of the fact that all of our decisions do not lead us to life. Many of our choices are destructive, confining, and wounding. Instead of promoting life, they plant seeds of internal death. These choices bring discontent, anxiety, incompleteness, ineffectiveness, self-centeredness, bitterness, and guilt. The issue, therefore, when we talk about dealing with our sexuality, is not violating rules but violating life and violating people. One wise person has observed that rules break, but people tear. What we want to avoid is tearing other people (and ourselves) in our expressions of our sexuality. These expressions of sexuality will either produce life or not produce life. The choice is ours.

This concept of sex being pro-life behavior may be difficult to understand. It is much easier for us to understand "right sex" and "wrong sex." Also, if we are ignoring our sexuality ("Whatever happens, happens!") or repressing it ("My sexuality is physical and therefore evil"), then "pro-life" makes no sense. Someone who is ignoring or repressing his or her sexuality has not yet integrated his or her sexuality—his or her body—into his or her person. That same individual would not understand that sitting next to someone on the bus—even a member of the same sex—is a sexual act because we can't do it without our body. Furthermore, the person who is ignoring or repressing has not yet been able to thank God for the gift of sexuality.

99

That last idea is worth emphasizing: sexuality *is* a gift. Sadly, few of us view it that way. Rather than regarding sexuality as a gift, "it remains for most men and women a world through which they move warily, cautiously, self-protectively—not a home but an alien land."[9] Not even married people automatically or thankfully accept sexuality as a gift to be enjoyed and celebrated. Hear what Dwight Small says:

> Sexual sanctity can easily be soiled outside of marriage; it can also be shopworn within marriage. The true nature and purpose of the sexual union can just as seriously be mismanaged inside of marriage as outside. Simply to keep sex for marriage is not sufficient to make it immune from tragedy and betrayal. Sex can be a sacrament or a sacrilege right within the marriage relation. It can be a hallowed thing or a hollow thing, a blessing or a burden. It is either a physical act from which there emerges a spiritual value, or it is a physical act and no more. Either it brings a deep sense of mutuality and oneness in love and trust, or it stands alone as a symbol of the ease with which two persons can exploit a pleasurable experience for purely selfish ends.[10]

When we—married or single—can't accept our sexuality as a gift, we can't be honest about our sexuality and therefore we don't take responsibility for ourselves. We end up playing a variety of games with our sexuality. Let's look at some of these games.

1. We become victims of our own freedom.

I define freedom as the possibility of choice. Just as we can become a slave to an identity package as we hide behind personages and depend on other people for a sense of worth, we can be enslaved by the patterns and consequences of the decisions we make about our sexuality. The specifics of Adam and Eve's situation clarify this point. They made a decision to disobey God. The resulting loss of innocence and feelings of guilt and shame prompted them to try to hide from God. This hiding would lead only to greater separation from God and further disobedience. Disobedience would increase the sense of guilt and shame and encourage more hiding—and you can see how the cycle works. The only thing that can break this cycle is confession. We need to acknowledge to God and to ourselves where we are making decisions which are not pro-life. Then we will be able to move on.

Although it is a fact of life that decisions have consequences, many people enter into sexual relationships thinking that they will be able to avoid any negative consequences. Sex seems to have become for some people a "vacation paradise into which supposedly anyone can venture successfully and without cost."[11] We enter a relationship with nothing down. We proceed to write checks with our body and emotions, assuming that the relationship will cost us nothing. All along, we fail to see the inevitable balloon payment at the end, and we eventually become a victim of our free choice to enter the relationship.[12]

In *The End of Sex*, one-time champion of free love George Leonard shares that he himself has learned this lesson: "What I have learned is that there are no games without rules."[13] In other words, there are consequences to our decisions and actions. If we don't choose wisely, the payment can be high.

One last note about this game. Our choices reveal who we are, but often we don't want to be owned by them. We don't want to take responsibility for ourselves. As long as that is true, we will be unable to accept our sexuality as a gift.

2. We redefine intimacy.

Remember the story of Edna and Bill from chapter 2? They used their sexuality as a way to avoid emotional and intellectual intimacy. Similarly, each one of us can use sexual

101

behavior to avoid and redefine intimacy. Men and women, for instance, tend to view intimacy differently. A man assumes that sex leads to intimacy: sexual activity means the presence of love and therefore the freedom to quit his journey toward intimacy. A woman, on the other hand, assumes that intimacy leads to sex: when she hears the words "I love you," a woman will feel an intimacy and is more agreeable to sexual activity. In neither instance is true intimacy experienced. Instead, as Rollo May once noted, "we've moved the fig leaf from our genitals to our face."[14] Because we are not skilled at intimacy, we hope that the physical involvement will prove to be an effective shortcut.

Again, let me refer back to the issue of what happens when I take responsibility for my own identity: I become dependent on you. Sex can play a key role in this pattern of dependence: I want you to like me, love me, and approve of me, so I give you my body. I now experience a sense of self-worth and something I can call "intimacy." Many of us, however, may be like the woman Eugene Peterson spoke with in chapter 8: "Sex was the only language she knew for describing relationships of intimacy."[15] The consequences of this are always unfulfilling and unfortunate.

3. We allow our emotions to become callous.

Loneliness, the fear of rejection, the reality of rejection, the lack of self-esteem, and many other things in life bring us pain. We want to avoid this pain, and sex often becomes an opportunity to soothe the pain we experience. Sex can cover up pain (I think again of Edna and Bill) and sex can help us deny our pain.

While sex can soothe our pain, the pain does not just disappear. Even though right now we may choose to ignore—or try to ignore—that pain, some day we will have to deal with it. In the meantime, though, we tend to build a wall around ourselves to protect us. Sex can help us in this construction project, but behind that wall, our emotions become callous.

4. We deify sex.

Like other false gods of materialism or success, sex promises more than it delivers. Nevertheless, our culture shouts to us the promises that good sex can lead to fulfillment, content-ment, and wholeness. Furthermore, these promises always emphasize performance or technique. People become mere objects. People are the pawns in the game called "Orgasm Is Life." The issue today is to achieve that climax—whatever the means. This focus desensitizes us to the reality that people who can be hurt are involved; this focus also robs us of the simple aspects of our sexuality. The significance of a hug is lost in the quest for the all-important orgasm.

Bombarded by society's messages about sex, how can we remove sex from the altar of a god? Listen to part of Ben Patterson's editorial: "Sex has always made extravagant claims for itself. Depending on who you listen to, it can send you to heaven or hell. Both are extravagant claims, and both are false. 'Contrary to Mrs. Grundy, sex is not sin,' says Frederick Buechner. 'Contrary to Hugh Hefner, it's not salva-tion either.' Sex is sex. It is human, nothing more and noth-ing less. . . . Like anything human, it is a gift from God filled with wonder and mystery. Also, like anything human, it is just that: human, mortal, ephemeral."[16]

Are you a slave in the free world of decisions about your sexuality? Are you playing games with your sexuality? As you consider those questions, let me leave you with a few closing thoughts.

First, we can't separate our body from our person. In this sense, all of life is sexual. If we let ourselves be honest about this fact, then we won't be tempted either to repress or ignore our sexuality. If we accept our bodies as bodies, we won't be intimidated by them. We will receive the gift of our sexuality from God: we won't see sex itself as god. The temptation, then, to make decisions which aren't pro-life will not be as strong.

Also, when we view sex as sex and sexuality as God's gift to us, we won't equate sexuality with intimacy. I will be able to take responsibility for my sexuality. The first step of acknowledging sexuality as a gift from God is important. Consider these words: "God, I thank You for creating me a body-person. Thank You for a body that works. Thank You for the sexual desires that I experience. Help me to see that sexuality is not something I need to deny or ignore. Help me to receive it as a gift from You."

Where, though, does this gift of our sexuality fit into our relationships? A diagram will help illustrate a healthy balance in life.

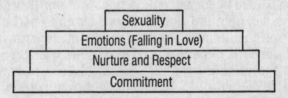

I see commitment to you—not to an active sex life—as the best foundation for our relationship. Built on that commitment—especially when that commitment takes place in the context of a commitment to God—can be a relationship of respect and love, and that will mean a healthy environment for sharing one's sexuality.

When I have made a commitment to you, I am free to nurture your growth as a person. I will not approach you as a taker: I won't need you to validate my worth as a person. I will be able to share my weaknesses. I will be able to be vulnerable, and I will be able to let you be vulnerable. I will be able to be open about my emotions, and I will be able to accept your expressions of your emotions. Only when we are willing to be honest about our relationships, only when we are willing to strive for a healthy balance, and only when we are willing to seek God's best for our relationships—only then will we be free to love each other and free to celebrate our sexuality as the special gift from God that it is.

Nothing is as important to a marriage as humility.

CHAPTER TEN

Intimate Marriages: Have We Settled for Less?

I still cringe when I think of my friend's remark. . . .

The day before one of my seminars on intimacy, I had run into Ted at a local church. "Are you going to my seminar?" I asked.

"What's it about?"

"Intimacy," I replied.

"Well," he grinned knowingly, "my wife is five months pregnant with our second child. I guess we have intimacy pretty much figured out!"

Unfortunately, Ted's perspective is not uncommon. As a culture, we tend to perpetuate the myth that marriage is a status synonymous with intimacy and that married people therefore have nothing else to learn about intimacy. I want to do whatever I can to destroy this myth that intimacy automatically comes with marriage. I also want to help you begin to experience a greater degree of intimacy in your marriage.

Many books have been written about this subject of marriage. I am certainly not intending for this chapter to be the final say. As I offer my perspective, though, I want to begin by defining marriage.

Marriage is more than a piece of paper, more than a social contract, more than a set of vows, more than permission to sleep with someone, and more than churches, tuxes, and gowns. Marriage is an institution designed to be a mirror that reflects how God loves His people. Consider these verses from Ephesians 5:

> . . . the husband is the head of the wife as Christ is the head of the church, his body, of which he is the Savior. . . . Husbands, love your wives, just as Christ loved the church and gave himself up for her. . . (verses 23, 25)

The intimate relationship which a marriage is intended to be is first described in Genesis 2:

> The man said,
> "This is now bone of my bones and flesh of my flesh;
> she shall be called 'woman,' for she was taken out of man."
> For this reason a man will leave his father and mother and be united to his wife, and they will become one flesh. (verses 23-24)

As the Bible teaches in these passages and in other places, when two people marry, they leave their homes, they cleave to one another, and they become one flesh. This three-step process reflects the love which Christ has for His church: Jesus came down from heaven, died for His church, and, as resurrected Lord, serves as head of the church. The love that His actions demonstrate can be reflected in the marriage of two people who truly do become one flesh.

Marriage is a unique relationship for another reason as well. In a marriage, the environment for nurture is based on a commitment of longevity. Although our friends do nurture us, they are free to reevaluate our relationship in five months or five years. I, however, am not free to reevaluate my relationship with Norva. I have put my life on the line with her. I have, to echo Genesis 2, made the vow to cleave and become one flesh. While other people in my life do nurture my growth as a person, my relationship with Norva is unique: we have made a vow that it will last.

110

Ironically, many people lay their life on the line with a rather casual "I do." They may never understand the significance of this step and they may never act as if they have truly invested their life in the other person. The vows we say, though, are statements of the fact that we are cutting one umbilical cord and tying ourselves to another person. The vows, to change the metaphor, are the means by which we write a check with our whole life. The "I do" reflects Christ's total and loving commitment to the church whether we like it or not and whether we do a very good job reflecting His love.

It is also important to note that marriage is holy. Before I explain, let me first emphasize that even though marriage is a holy state, it is not the ultimate condition of intimacy and it is not the goal that each one of us should be striving for in our life. Even Paul, who advised in 1 Corinthians 7 that single people stay single, talks about the holiness of marriage.

A marriage is holy and unique because it is so covenantal: by design, marriage is a life-long covenant. This covenant is another reflection of God and His love for His people.[1] From the time of Noah, our God has been a God of covenants; from the time of Abraham, these covenants were specifically redemptive in both content and purpose. These covenants were built on the promise of Leviticus 26:12—"I will walk among you and be your God, and you will be my people." Likewise, a marriage covenant is a promise of faithfulness and love. The two people vow to stand with each other for life; they pledge to one another a love which will help nurture them in the way of the Lord.

Marriage, therefore, being a relationship held in such high esteem by God, should never be a situation in which people are settling for second best. Marriage partners should instead be experiencing an exciting and fulfilling intimacy as they share their lives with each other.

Think for a moment of marriage as a journey towards this kind of intimacy. Let me now offer certain key ideas which can serve as signposts to help you make the journey. These ideas can be woven into the fabric of marriage, and so help you and your mate move toward a richer relationship.

1. Let humility be your guide.

At a recent seminar, a man kept asking me for the one secret to a healthy marriage. I told him that I didn't believe that there is just one element which will guarantee a healthy, long-lasting marriage, but he kept insisting. Finally I obliged him a one-word answer—"Humility."

It was a spur of the moment response, but the more I've thought about it, the more I like that answer. Nothing is as important to a marriage as humility.

- Humility is the spirit of receiving.
- Humility does not rely on guarantees for relational security.
- Humility is the attitude which regards life and love as gifts.

The attitude that life is a gift focuses a person on the gift of a single day, and it is this focus which can build intimacy and strengthen a marriage.

We all want guarantees for security. We want the feeling of having arrived at something stable and lasting. This "something" is, for many of us, marriage. "I do," however, does not mean "I am done—I am finished—I have arrived." "I do" instead means that I'm committing myself to work on this relationship and that I will work on it daily. I will make my marriage look like the fulfillment of a lifetime covenant *today*. I am not guaranteed tomorrow, much less a fiftieth wedding anniversary. I do have today, though, and I will work on my marriage today.

Consider three other aspects of humility.

- Humility is the awareness that in and of myself I cannot give complete meaning to this relationship.

112

- Humility is an honesty about my own weaknesses and shortcomings.
- Humility is open to learning new things; it is open to change and growth.

As we've seen before in this book, we cannot define our own self-worth. Neither can we assign meaning or significance to our relationships. God offers us worth, and He also offers meaning for our relationships. Once God is part of my life and my marriage, I can rest in Him. I can trust Him for the relationship. As a result of that trust, I can let go of fears of rejection which would cause me to hide. Also, once God is part of my marriage, I will see myself in contrast to Him. My weaknesses and shortcomings will become apparent, but as I trust Him and His love for me, I will be able to both accept myself and share myself with my mate. This same realization of my weaknesses can encourage me to learn new things; it can spur me on to change and growth.

Humility, with its precious spirit of receiving, keeps my focus on God, the source of the gift of life and love. Humility therefore helps me always keep my priorities in check by prompting me to consider whether I am striving today to live out my covenant of love for my mate. Finally, humility reintroduces into my life the elements of wonder and awe—elements which lead to freedom and joy.

2. Marriage is not a competitive sport.

If I have difficulty bringing an attitude of genuine humility into our marriage, I will place great demands on you: I will need you to complete me, I will need you to define the relationship, and I will need you to guarantee the relationship. I will be taking my unhealthy dependence into our marriage. When this dependence is brought into a relationship, everything is based on performance—and suddenly we're competitors.

When I depend on you, for instance, to make the relationship okay, you need to perform in certain ways for me. At the same time, I fear your thoughts and opinions of me, so I perform in ways which I think you will find acceptable. Both of us will be striving towards certain standards of performance, and performance reports will become our way of keeping score. Although we never seem to perform up to the proper standards, we have bought into the idea that it is necessary for us to perform. It becomes more important to *do* things which make me a good husband than to *give* to Norva; it becomes more important to *demand* that Norva do things than to *receive* from her. In the midst of all these performance reports, we miss the journey of life. We get bogged down, and we neglect the journey towards intimacy.

This competitive spirit is reflected in what psychologists claim is the number one reason for marital breakups—anger. Not surprisingly, anger comes when frustrations build up: "You can't perform well enough for me. I need reassurance and guarantees." This hurt and disappointment soon become anger. As the diagram on the next page illustrates, there are four ways in which we can deal with this anger. Look at the options and the various consequences. The fourth way is the healthy way—and it is this healthy step of forgiveness which breaks the pattern of competition and frees us to move on.

Competition in a marriage relationship is like any other competition: as competitors, we are often wounded. We experience disappointment from unmet expectations, pain from unrealistic or unnecessary demands, hurts from misunderstandings, and loneliness from the lack of honest communication. Forgiveness is the gift from God that helps us deal with these wounds. Forgiveness is the gift from God which frees us from competition.

4. Forgiveness

Anger is acknowledged and then surrendered to God. Only forgiveness leads to honest and open communication; only forgiveness leads to the freedom to enjoy a relationship of love and intimacy.

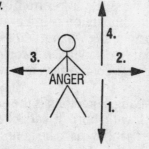

2. Blame

Anger is pushed outward. Blaming you increases competition and causes me more pain.

3. Ignoring

Anger is pushed against a wall. The dishonest conclusion of ignoring is a false sense that I'm okay— "Angry? Not me!"

1. Repression

My anger is pushed down inside. Denying anger—"Hurt? What hurt?"—leads to dishonesty and ulcers.

Before looking at what forgiveness is and what it isn't, consider this situation:

Norva: "I was hoping that we could spend some time talking tonight."

Terry: "Okay."

Norva: "I'm concerned about the way we've communicated lately. I'm feeling ignored by you."

Terry: "You know, that reminds me of that time when we were on vacation last year, and you were mad at me and didn't talk to me."

What does this conversation illustrate? First, notice how the discussion became competition. Neither of us could receive (i.e., listen) and neither of us could give (i.e., let the other person talk honestly about a frustration or concern). This kind of conversation tends to be a game of one-upmanship: "I have to be one up on you—and you didn't listen either!" In competition like this, feeling like a superior competitor becomes more important than feeling loved. Forgiveness can change this.

First, let me say that forgiveness sets us free from competition because it declares that competition is irrelevant. Forgiveness teaches me that competition will not add anything to my identity or my self-worth. In competition, I would never be free of performance standards. Forgiveness, however, can be the great emancipator.

- Forgiveness is not forgetting. Forgetting is the amputation method of dealing with hurt. It cannot lead to growth because it does not allow us to be honest about where we are now or about what we are feeling.
- Forgiveness is not ignoring. The "okay-it-doesn't-matter-anyway" approach is only another form of repression. It works on paper and perhaps in our minds, but our stomach pays the price.
- Forgiveness is not a magic formula. Many people, though, hope to avoid looking at real issues by reciting the "Oh, I'm sorry" or "That's okay! I forgive you!" formula.

Neither forgetting, ignoring, or reciting certain words is a realistic or healthy way of dealing with hurt. None of these options is an act of forgiveness. Real forgiveness must take place in the real world, and it must deal honestly with problems that come in life. Forgiveness says, though, "I surrender my right to hurt you back."[2] Forgiveness says, "I give up my right and my desire to keep score."

When I don't forgive, I become like a squirrel storing up chestnuts for the winter. Someday I will go back to this or that reminder of a time you hurt me, and I'll get even with you! Also, when I don't forgive, I let my identity be defined by the hurts I've experienced. I cling to memories which can easily become self-fulfilled prophecies: I set myself up for hurt in other situations by expecting to be hurt. Finally, as my conversation with Norva pointed out, lack of forgiveness leads to hurling. I become defensive and say things which are hurtful and destructive. When I am feeling defensive, communication is a mere exercise in futility. Forgiveness, though, frees us from all these things. Forgiveness frees us from our need to collect chestnuts. Forgiveness frees us from these tendencies to cling to past hurts and to lash out at people we care about. How, though, can we forgive?

• Acknowledge the hurt.

As we've learned in other situations, unless we are honest about what we are feeling, we can't move on. When the issue is forgiveness, we begin by acknowledging the hurt that we have experienced.

• Remind yourself of who owns you.

Remind yourself that your identity is intact in the hands of a loving and faithful God. Your identity is not affected by the number of chestnuts you collect: those chestnuts cannot make you better or more loved.

• Forgiveness is a *choice*—an act of the will, not an emotion.

It is important to realize that you may never feel like forgiving the person who hurt you. Even without those feelings, though, the step of forgiveness can be taken. You simply need to decide to forgive that person. Make the decision to free yourself from being shackled to the hurt you're feeling. Free yourself to move forward and grow.

• Forgiveness is slow.

Like taking vitamins, forgiveness needs to be a daily act. Like aerobics, forgiveness requires consistency, practice, effort, and time. Jesus taught that we are to forgive the same hurt seventy times seven times (Matthew 18:21-22). True forgiveness cannot be rushed or hurried.

• Forgiveness requires reinforcement.

This reinforcement can come in the form of positive affirmations which you tell yourself regularly. Remind yourself consistently that you have forgiven the one who hurt you. Reinforce for yourself the fact that you are giving up the right to hurt that person back. This kind of talk will confirm your choice to forgive the person.

• Forgiveness begins with you.

In more direct words, *you* start first! Don't wait for the other person to make the move. Don't use forgiveness as a club— "Aren't you lucky that I'm forgiving you!" Instead, make the decision to forgive and then forgive the person, knowing all the while that this forgiveness is something you are doing for yourself. You are freeing yourself from the past.

3. Remember your covenant.

I heard Lewis Smedes make an interesting and wise comment in a lecture he gave: "Over the past twenty-plus years, my wife has been married to five different men—and all of them have been me."[3] The point he makes so well is that we all change. Change is inevitable. The marriage covenant is the framework for dealing with this change.

I often hear in my counseling sessions the comment that, "She's not the person I married." Of course not! Her husband's frustration is understandable when we realize that he, like the rest of us, wants a guarantee in our relationship. A covenant is not a guarantee. A covenant is not a commitment to a particular personality. A covenant is, however, a "commitment to a direction."[4]

If I don't understand the importance of the covenant I have made with my spouse, then I will be tempted by chemistry—and our culture encourages this. We have all heard the message that if our eyes connect with another person in just the right way, it must be love. When I got married, though, I got married for the covenant, not for the chemistry. Chemistry does not a relationship make. Chemistry also doesn't deny the marriage covenant I have made. It is important to remember again and again this covenant you have made with your spouse. It will help you keep your focus on the relationship that you have committed yourself to for life.

4. Respect your spouse: he or she is not your servant.

If I enter our marriage with a misunderstanding of my identity and of the source of my self-worth, I will be entering the relationship with the expectation that you will make me okay. In other words, I married you to do that task and you, therefore, are my servant. The consequences can only be disastrous.

If, however, I create in our marriage an environment of nurture, I'll see you as God's servant. I may even be able to look at you with a sense of wonder. My purpose will be to create an environment where your Master, Jesus Christ, can work in you. If I base my respect for you on the idea that you are my servant, I won't be able to respect you when you don't

119

perform up to my expectations (when you don't, for instance, lose weight). My respect should instead be based on the fact that God created you. As one of His unique and precious creatures, you deserve my respect and love.

5. Fight fairly.

Many people respond negatively to the word "fight." This reaction is probably reinforced by whatever philosophy for handling obstacles, disagreements, and problems that you—and everyone in this world—have. There is no such thing as life without conflicts, so every person undoubtedly has a philosophy about how to cope with them. Consider these popular options:

- "We seldom have disagreements. As a matter of fact, I don't even remember the last one."
- "Conflict? What conflict?"
- "Yes, we disagree, but I'm usually right."
- "It's more loving for me not to talk about it. I wouldn't want to hurt him/her."

Another popular way of thinking about conflict is to assume that once we've worked through that problem or once we're past this set of inconveniences, our marriage will be better. We will be on a course of smooth sailing. This "When . . . then . . ." way of thinking is just one more way of avoiding the conflict. Furthermore, marriage—just like life itself—is not the absence of obstacles, inconveniences, or conflict. Those things *are* your marriage; they are your life and they are my life. Smooth sailing does not a marriage make. Smooth sailing does make for two very bored people.

Since conflict cannot be avoided, it is important that you and your mate have a covenant for conflict resolution or, to use that electric word, a covenant for fighting. We'll look at this issue more closely in chapter 12, but here are some general guidelines:

- Use "I" statements rather than "you" statements. ("I feel hurt when you . . ." rather than "You hurt me when you . . .")
- In the middle of resolving the conflict, don't leave the room.
- Don't sleep on your anger.
- Don't strike or hit the other person.
- Don't reprimand the other person in public.

One more word about conflict as it relates to the issue of intimacy. It is my belief that intimacy is never real in isolation: it only comes alive over and against something. Specifically, Norva only knows that I love her in the midst of conflict or when I listen despite my own inconvenience. Without conflict, my love would never be acted out, and intimacy would not and could not exist.

As I close this discussion of marriage, let me say one more time that marriage is not the only relationship where intimacy can exist. Because of the unique environment of a marriage relationship, because of its nature that reflects the relationship between Christ and the church, because of its commitment to longevity—because of all these things, marriage is a fertile ground for the nurturing of intimacy. I would urge you not to take such fertile ground for granted. Take care of the fragile roots of intimacy which flower in a marriage. The fruit that your care will bring you is well worth the hard work.

*When we pay the price of taking risks,
we are free to emerge from behind walls
we had hoped would keep us secure.*

CHAPTER ELEVEN

What Will It Cost Me?

I ntimacy is an aerobic activity. Let me explain. Just as physical fitness doesn't happen instantly or effortlessly, intimacy does not happen easily. There is no magical potion. There are no three easy steps to immediate results. There is no lasting state of intimacy without regular maintenance. Not to understand these facts is to settle for something far less than intimacy. Not to understand these facts may mean secretly wishing for that day when our relationships will be magically transformed to something more than they are today.

I struggled with such a desire for this "something more," and one of my journal entries reveals the frustration I felt: "So, having said a hearty 'Amen,' I plunged headlong into a relationship I called 'intimate.' In a few months or weeks (or was it minutes?), I came back home to lick my wounds. I soon assumed a new battle slogan and increased my defense budget. Having before secured my fortress and deemed it impenetrable, I was surprised (or was I?) to find myself once again licking my wounds and crying to the tune of 'Alone Again—Naturally.' Relationships—who needs them?"

Think for a moment of this life we lead as a supermarket of sorts, and then consider how much time we spend in the section called "Relationships." There we grab for the various packages labeled "Intimacy." As we fill our cart as quickly as possible, we are still very much aware and quite envious of those people who seem able to fill their carts more quickly than we can. Glad to have at least something to show for our efforts, though, we rush to the exit and hope that we'll be able to enjoy our new purchases. But, conveniently perhaps, we have forgotten one thing in our hurry to get to the door. In order to leave, we must pass the checkout counter where we will be asked to pay for those packages piled high in our cart. Pay? Oh yes—but we never even thought to look at the price tags!

Intimacy is not free. Intimacy will cost us something. Are we willing to pay the price? First we need to know what the cost will be. What price must I pay in order to fully understand vulnerability and take the risk of peeling back one corner of my personage? Also, where did the assumption that intimacy is inexpensive come from? How is it that we are led to believe that intimacy serendipitously occurs apart from our need to pay a price?

In response to the last question, let me suggest that we have been raised on two unfortunate assumptions regarding intimacy. Both are perpetuated by the media, both are offered as hope, and both are false.

First, our culture argues that intimacy results from a person's need for attention and admiration. This emphasis on appearance and performance leads to the inaccurate idea that intimacy comes instantly upon evaluation and approval of certain externals—and this idea is pure fantasy. Intimacy involves what is internal, and therefore achieving intimacy takes time as we slowly choose to risk sharing our person.

Our culture also argues that intimacy will be free of any form of pain—and we readily accept this idea. Consider the hour-long television programs in which two people meet, fall in love, establish a relationship, and develop "intimacy." This intimacy which comes quickly and painlessly teaches the lesson that pain is an option—an option to be avoided! Furthermore, if I assume that intimacy will be painless I feel I must repress any and every sign of pain or conflict—an approach that is neither healthy nor honest. Not wanting to experience pain, though, we tend to welcome the idea (as false as it is) that intimacy is painless.

Contrary, then, to what our society teaches, intimacy is more than receiving strokes for externals and intimacy will involve some pain. Intimacy requires more than finding the most attractive package and going home to enjoy it. As I've said, there is a price to intimacy, and we must ask ourselves whether we are willing to pay it. Let's look together at seven price tags.

Price Tag #1: An Honest Self-Image

Many people wonder what this has to do with intimacy or why this is considered a cost. These people think of learning about intimacy as learning how to find the right person, how to understand that person, and how to win that person's love. The inability to develop an honest self-image, however, will directly affect a person's ability to develop mature relationships. The two are unquestionably intertwined. But what *is* an honest self-image? How can we develop an honest self-image? And how can we know where we have fallen short?

A good starting point in considering these questions is Romans 12:3. There Paul writes, "Do not think of yourself more highly than you ought, but think of yourself with sober judgment." Until recently, I had assumed that Paul's statement did not apply to me. After all, I was certainly not suffering from thinking of myself too highly. I have since learned differently. My problem was—and often still is—a low sense of self-worth or low self-esteem—and this is common to most of us. I needed people's approval. I needed to build my self-worth on strokes I got from them.

With these feelings of low self-worth, whom did I focus on? The answer, of course, was myself, and I realized the irony of low self-worth. Poor self-esteem causes us to focus our

127

energy and attention on ourselves. In other words, I was preoccupied with *me*, and such preoccupation with self is a guaranteed obstacle to intimacy.

If we decide to work toward intimacy by paying this first price, what do we do to develop an honest view of ourselves? What *is* an honest self-image? Simply put, an honest self-image is an accurate self-image. It is built on something more than my own preoccupation with myself. It means seeing myself as I am seen by the One who knows me best. It is understanding my identity through the eyes of my Creator. It is recognizing who really owns me.

If I am unable to give up an obsessive preoccupation with self, though, I will find myself subject to two immediate temptations. First, I will begin to view others not as people, but as objects. As we mentioned in chapter 7, everything around me will become something which may eventually make me okay. My ability to really care for you will be severely handicapped by my need for you to make me acceptable.

I will also tend to sabotage relationships from the very start. This happens as an extension of my poor self-image: if I have difficulty finding the worth in myself, how can I believe that you will find it? Such an attitude (however conscious or unconscious) and the resulting actions fit the classic approval-avoidance pattern. First, because I need you to make me okay, I will draw very close to you (or as close as I know how). Then, because of the fear that you will not find in me someone worth loving (because *I* don't find someone worth loving), I intentionally set the relationship up for failure.

This first price tag of an honest self-image calls for a payment that is important but difficult. One reason for the difficulty is our record of past mistakes. When we fail in relationships, we ourselves make such convenient scapegoats. As one woman said through her tears, "I just know no one can love me. Every time I give myself to people—both male and female—they use me and then discard me. I must be worth very little." Unfortunately, that woman carried this image of herself into each one of her relationships, and each outcome could have been predicted. The self-image became self-fulfilled prophecy. Furthermore, her self-pity will keep her from ever needing to face—head on—her own responsibility in this pattern of broken relationships.

In the preface to this book, I quoted a passage from the gospel of Luke that applies here. Those verses told of Jesus' desire to set captives free. People with low self-esteem are captives who need to be set free. They are captives who need to hear the declaration of the Liberator, captives who need to hear that their worth is not dependent on the past, on their record of success and failure, or on their ability to perform. Instead, their self-worth—like yours and mine—is dependent upon the Liberator alone.

As we saw in chapter 7, God's love does liberate me when I choose to live as if what He says about me is true. Ironically, if I can be truly liberated, I slowly find that my need for another person is diminished. I am complete, and as a complete person, I am free to choose to relate to you because of who you are and not because you may be just what I need to be a whole person. The purpose of a relationship is not to derive love—and I won't have that selfish motivation if my identity is in God. If I don't need to take from you in order to be okay, then I'm truly free to give all that there is of me. The first step towards this freedom is looking honestly at myself in the light of God's love.

Price Tag #2 : A Relationship with God

In paying that first price, I will realize that an honest self-image comes when I hear the voice of One who truly knows me and who loves me despite that complete knowledge of me. This is the beginning of a relationship with God—a relationship that is important to any relationship we have with another human being. Let me explain.

If I see no purpose in life that is greater than myself, then our relationship will need to be defined by you and me. I believe that such a relationship is destined to be one of frustration and disappointment as we fail to perform up to each other's standards. If, however, you and I recognize God's love for us, we will have found purpose and significance. We will be two whole people who are able to share ourselves freely with each other. We will still frustrate and disappoint each other, but we will have a basis for dealing with those situations. If I believe what God says about me, I will be learning what He believes about and feels for you as well. What God says therefore gives you value, too. His words and His love for us give significance to our relationship with each other.

The fact is that all of us need a purpose greater than ourselves to give significance to our relationships—and this is not a particularly religious statement. People, however religious they are or aren't, seek a purpose in life that is greater than they themselves. That purpose has a variety of labels such as "humanitarian" or "for the public good." For me, the purpose greater than myself is God and His statement of love for me. In His love, I find my identity.

The symbol of the triangle is helpful here.

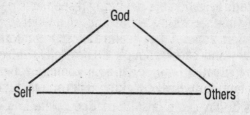

130

My relationship with another person is symbolized by the horizontal line. To free ourselves from preoccupation with self (and therefore with taking), we need the vertical relationship. This vertical relationship with God gives meaning to the horizontal, and the outcome is reflected in the symbol. As two people grow closer to God, they of necessity grow closer to one another. Growing closer to God means acquiring an honest self-image, understanding another person's value, and finding purpose and significance in life—three elements which I see as essential to intimacy.

Price Tag #3 : Risk

"Isn't there a way to find intimacy without having to expose to you who I am?" My friend's question is not only legitimate—it is also very common. *Is* there any way to experience intimacy without having to take some risks? Is risk always a prerequisite to relationships? It seems that we're all secretly hoping that the other person will choose to be intimate with us first. I hope that she will take the first step because I know all too well that the first step *I* take would move me beyond my comfort zone.

My comfort zone is built around that area of myself and my life that I believe I must protect and defend. Risk, then, is the step of self-disclosure at which I share these private areas of my life, and such risk taking must be a responsible behavior. What many people call "risk," however, is in fact quite irresponsible behavior. People, for instance, who return again and again to relationships where they know there will be abuse and rejection are not being responsible risk takers. Ironically, this returning again and again only reinforces one's comfort zone. A key feature of any comfort zone is familiarity—and sadly enough a completely miserable or unhealthy situation can serve as a comfort zone. Staying with this familiarity makes taking risks an even more difficult thing to do.

Even responsible risks, though, can be difficult and will seem quite costly. I can feel so protective of my fragile identity that I will be afraid to let you know me. I will fear your judgment of me. If I reveal a little of who I am to you, you could very well choose to reject me. To avoid this rejection, I simply avoid risk. Again, the pattern appears. We hide behind a mask because we fear that the real us will be rejected. We also live according to the myth that intimacy can be exempt from pain. Since the risk of sharing could involve some pain, I choose to avoid risk.

There is another kind of pain, though, which needs to be addressed, and that is the pain of regret. To avoid any and all risk is to confine ourselves to our comfort zone, but it is also sentencing ourselves to the pain of regret. Having not given anything of ourselves, we've never had the opportunity to receive. Neither have we experienced the joy that comes with watching another receive. The pain of regret can be a haunting, lingering ache. As you consider the choice between the possible pain of risk and the pain of regret, listen to the wise words of C. S. Lewis:

> To love at all is to be vulnerable. Love anything, and your heart will certainly be wrung and possibly be broken. If you want to make sure of keeping it intact, you must give your heart to no one, not even to an animal. Wrap it carefully around with hobbies and little luxuries; avoid all entanglements; lock it up safe in the casket or coffin of your selfishness. But in that casket—safe, dark, motionless, airless—it will change. It will not be broken; it will become unbreakable, impenetrable, irredeemable. The alternative to tragedy, or at least to the risk of tragedy, is damnation. The only place outside Heaven where you can be perfectly safe from all the dangers and perturbations of love is Hell.[1]

Lewis's words are an eloquent expression of a profound and very real truth. We can only experience life when we take a risk. We can only be fully alive when we don't try to protect ourselves.

Price Tag #4: Honesty about the Possibility of Pain

If I choose to peel back one corner of my mask, you can respond in one of two ways: you can accept me or reject me. (And there is something in all of us that wants one of those choices eliminated!) Is there any way that your acceptance of me can be guaranteed? One man expressed his frustration at a seminar: "Why are you even saying that rejection is an alternative? Who in his right mind would choose to live with hurt, grief, emotional bruises, scars, and pain?"

I understand his feelings, but the issue here is not that of *choosing* rejection. The issue is facing the reality that the risk of rejection—and therefore pain—is inherent in one person's freedom to care about another. With free choice, there is the possibility of pain. Only when a person is free to leave you, however, is that person free to stay with you. Just as light has meaning to me only because I have been in darkness and health brings peace only because I have known sickness, that person's staying has meaning only because of his or her freedom to leave. To avoid any possibility of pain, then, is to water down intimacy. To seek a guarantee is to remove the very heart of freedom. Love merely becomes an activity to be carried out by robots.

The implication here is not that we seek pain; we are not advocating some form of masochism. When we willingly and honestly face this price tag, though, we discover that pain need not be an enemy to intimacy. The possibility of pain does not cheapen intimacy. On the contrary, truly intimate behaviors come only in the face of freedom and therefore the possibility of pain. The richness of intimacy comes when you take the risk of being rejected and hurt and you find yourself accepted instead.

If you take the risk and pain results, face that pain. View the pain as an affirmation that you are fully alive. Consider, for instance, that for a patient lying in a hospital room after surgery, pain means life. In a similar way, emotional pain means life. Consider that tears would make no sense except that they signal pain. Likewise, "I'm sorry" is meaningless without the presence of pain. An embrace makes no sense if we don't know the absence of the embrace and the pain of that aloneness. Most important, the Resurrection makes no sense without the horror and pain of the Cross. Pain is a signal of the presence of life. It is also a signal that resurrection is possible.

Although none of us likes pain, I would still encourage you to risk experiencing pain by taking the risk of sharing yourself with another person. If you are accepted, the risk will have been worthwhile. If you are hurt, let me reassure you that you need not be alone with your pain. God will be with you. He doesn't guarantee us a life free from pain, but He does promise to be with us always (Matthew 28:20).

God has become real to me not when He has protected me from life's pain and trials, but when He has shown Himself to me in the midst of those difficult times. When He reminds me that He owns me with all my fears, my insecurities, my need for guarantees, and my longing for love, then He becomes in a very real way the God of unconditional and sustaining love. The possibility of experiencing pain in relationships is very real—but so is the promise of God's presence and peace.

Price Tag #5 : Time

We live in a microwave society where all things are possible in less than sixty minutes. Leaving a theatre not long ago, for instance, I realized that I had just watched two complete strangers meet, fall in love, develop a sex life, get married, have children, and live through several severe crises—all in less than two hours. Subconsciously, I apply—and probably you do as well—that sense of time to my relationships: I want intimacy—and I want it now!

Our culture reinforces this unrealistic concept of time. Consider the lie that ecstatic moments are the bond of intimacy. We want to fall in love with fireworks and Ravel's "Bolero" playing in the background. A high premium is placed on experiencing ecstatic emotions. We therefore spend a lot of energy taking our "intimacy temperature" and we depend greatly on the way we *feel* about another person. This emphasis on joyful intoxication is at the heart of a battle we are destined to lose. We can't win because it seems that we can never do enough to generate and maintain the right level of emotional intensity—at least, we can never do what we see on television!

Underlying this desire for ecstatic and continual bliss is a misunderstanding about the role that time plays in the development of an intimate relationship. We want life to happen the way it does in the movies. We want—if not expect—the words, the glances, and the smiles to be just right. The things which maintain a relationship, though, are not the result of immediate and magical encounters with another person. The exhilarating moments, the "ah-ha's," the belly laughter, the tears—all of these times depend upon a sustained history of personal covenant for their meaning.[2] That covenant of relationship—that covenant of intimacy—needs a lot of care, attention, nurture, and, yes, time. The tears and laughter of a new relationship are superficial in comparison to the tears and laughter that have been seasoned by time.

Price Tag #6: Personal Responsibility and Accountability

Up to this point, we have discussed five price tags, all of which focus on our personal responsibility in an intimate relationship. The fact remains, though, that by definition a relationship involves two people.

I had a conversation with a young woman who seemed completely frustrated by her inability to stay in an intimate relationship. Her comments reflected her frustration: "I agree with you about the price tags. But what if the person I am in a relationship with doesn't care about them? Intimacy can't be a one-person show, can it?"

I understand her dilemma. It is true that for intimacy to have any meaning, there must be mutuality. But that leads me to share two observations before I discuss the subject of accountability.

First, I must act on the premise that intimate behaviors in my relationships always begin with me. All too often I wait for you to take the risk of sharing. I wait for you to initiate the conversation which will encourage me to be honest or vulnerable. And when you don't do so—or at least when you don't to *my* satisfaction—I begin to resent you. I angrily cry to myself, "You're not coming through with your end of the bargain!"

I often hear people make this remark: "We would have a wonderful relationship if only he/she would show more sensitivity"—or concern, or love, or something else. This statement may be true, but a more important point must be made. If I place the burden of our relationship on you, I will soon discover that you can never seem to do enough to please me. I need to be responsible for our relationship. I can't blame you for not, by yourself, making the relationship all that I want it to be. Intimate behaviors, therefore, must begin with me.

Second, I must *not* assume that you see the relationship the same way I do. There is only one way to find out the other person's perspective—ask! While that sounds like obvious advice, we don't always act on it. In a conversation with a lady in her mid-thirties, for instance, I asked about her current dating relationship. She replied, "I expect that we will be talking about marriage soon." Not long after that I spoke with the man involved. His response to the same question? "It's been fun, but I'll certainly never see her as anything more than a friend." And we wonder why intimacy often appears to be a one-person show! Intimacy doesn't have a chance when we don't communicate!

Now, having seen the need to be an initiator and an inquirer, let's consider more closely the price tag of accountability. Let me begin with this claim: the possibility of experiencing intimacy is directly related to the degree to which two people find themselves accountable to clear expectations for their relationship.

Everyone enters relationships with expectations. Unfortunately, few of these ideas are ever verbalized and many are subconscious. Perhaps we are afraid to verbalize expectations for in doing so we may be disappointed or even rejected. Assuming, then, that it's better to say nothing, we simply hope for the best.

"But 'expectations' suggests 'strings attached," said one young man at a recent seminar, "and I want to love someone with no strings attached." That sounds noble and romantic—and unrealistic. All of us expect certain things in a relationship, and pretending otherwise won't accomplish anything. It is, once again, our need for comfort and security that prevents us from being open about these expectations. We fear that we may drive the other person away, so we opt for silence or even dishonesty. John Powell makes this observation: "Most of us feel that others will not tolerate such emotional honesty in communication. We would rather defend our dishonesty on the grounds that it [our honesty] might hurt others; and, having rationalized our phoniness into nobility, we settle for superficial relationships."[3]

Interestingly enough, our silence or inability to be up front with our expectations will only hurt us. Inevitably, as the relationship goes on, we will realize that we are sacrificing many of our expectations—some of which may be legitimate. We have instead chosen not to share our hopes and ideas for fear of hurting the other person. The more we sacrifice, however, the more we begin to resent the other person and we blame him/her for our dissatisfaction with the relationship.

The idea that silence or dishonesty is better than an honesty that might hurt someone is only one fallacy we have accepted. We have also been conned into believing that obstacles, conflicts, frustration, expectations, and suffering are all of necessity enemies to intimacy. Believing that myth, we don't let ourselves notice any sign of their existence. The price tag called accountability, however, says that I do not have to allow conflict or other obstacles to become a threat to my ability to be intimate. Accountability says that I am putting myself on the line and am asking you to do the same. In the next chapter, we'll look at ways to deal with the conflicts that can arise when two people value honesty in their relationship. Again, that honesty is a fundamental aspect of the price tag of accountability.

Let me say that I am convinced that without this commitment to accountability we are destined to superficiality in our relationships. In Ephesians, Paul writes of "speaking the truth in love" (4:15). Honesty and integrity are at stake here. To not speak the truth in love is to sacrifice truth for comfort, convenience, or immediacy. Furthermore, love seeks your best interest and, in turn, my best interest. To deny you my honesty is not in your best interest. Neither is it loving for me to perpetuate an unhealthy situation: it isn't loving for me to let us remain stuck to our need to be secure rather than pushing us to be honest with one another. If our motto is, "Let's not rock the boat," then together we sink.

Now that we better understand the concept of accountability, where do we begin to act? Start by thinking about some of your relationships. On a piece of paper, list them and two or three expectations you have for each. Are these expectations realistic or unrealistic? Are they based on love or selfishness? Are you willing to express them to the person with whom you are in relationship?

Expectations are not demands and must not be expressed as such. Demands are "shoulds" which require the other person to change to our liking before we give our seal of approval. Instead, expectations are wishes which communicate our honest feelings and ideas regarding what we are willing to give to the relationship and what we would like to receive in return. Expectations help us define the degree to which both of us are committed to the relationship.

Invariably, someone will approach me with the following question: "I'm in a relationship where there have been both verbal and physical expressions of commitment. At one point, though, I took a risk and shared a sensitive issue. His/her response was to laugh! I thought that we had an intimate relationship! Now what do I do?" In dealing with this kind of reaction, one temptation is to forget about the hurt. "I'll get over it," I tell myself. I might choose to get even—"He/she had no right to treat me that way!"—or to withdraw—"That will be the last time I ever share anything with her/him!" Obstacles and conflict have thus become a barrier to my intimacy.

Accountability, however, says that I can and should face the conflict head on. Accountability also says that I can go to the person who has offended me and, in love, say, "Because I care about you and about our relationship, I want to share my feelings with you. I am feeling hurt (or angry or whatever) by your remarks, and I find myself wanting to hurt you back. I don't want to follow through on that desire. I want to understand you. And I want you to hear me and understand me."

Such an expression of honesty is a very intimate behavior: it is peeling back a corner of your mask and revealing who you are. Also, as the example illustrates, accountability does not involve "you" statements. The emphasis is not on blame—"*You* did this!" or "*You* made me do that!"—but on the honest expression of what *I* am thinking or feeling.

Are we always able to live up to these standards and expectations? No, not always. We do fail, but it is accountability that provides us a common ground for dealing with our failures. The price tag of accountability is a statement of purpose and an outline of the parameters of the relationship. If that sounds stifling or confining, consider this study of playground behavior. Psychologists decided to remove the fences from around the schoolyard: they felt that the fences limited the children's freedom. When the fences were down, though, the children played in a huddle in the center of the yard. Not knowing where they could play, they didn't venture from the center. When the fences were put up again, the children played throughout the playground. This study vividly illustrates what accountability can do for us: when we put fences up—when we honestly outline our expectations and define our commitment—then we can experience freedom.

Price Tag #7 : Perseverance

I don't know if you've been counting, but perseverance is the seventh price tag we have looked at. Intimacy is getting to be expensive!

It is also quite likely that this picture of intimacy can appear highly idealized and quite possibly unattainable. Intimate relationships may seem too abstract or even impossible to grasp. Such a conclusion is very understandable, but it is not necessarily accurate. Intimacy does not happen instantly, but it does happen. As it happens, the price tags wax and wane in their importance. The same price tag which seems critical at one time may soon fade into the background. Another price tag may not even be an issue for some people. The price tags are not organized as a ladder to intimacy. The progress toward intimacy is unique to a given relationship at a given time. This movement is a process that takes time—and that's where Price Tag #7 is important.

Perseverance is *not* gritting one's teeth during this journey toward intimacy. Neither am I referring to an inability to end a relationship because of the fear of impending guilt. Perseverance instead is the ability to say, "I will not quit this process toward intimacy because there is Someone who will not quit on me." Who is that Someone? My Creator. My Owner. My Lord. My God. He has shown Himself to me, and He confirms His love and acceptance of me regardless of what I do or fail to do. I need to hear that again and again. Why? Because I am tempted to feel frustrated by my inability to pay, immediately or consistently, the seven-part cost of intimacy. But God has never asked me—or us—to achieve something in order for Him to love us. In fact, He loves us regardless of whether we achieve or not. (See Psalm 89:33; Jeremiah 31:3; Ephesians 2:4; and 2 Thessalonians 2:16.)

This fact of God's love and faithfulness means that we are off the hook! We have been set free! We are free to choose one small intimate behavior. We are free to pay one small price. We are free to love apart from any need to prove ourselves.

- When we pay the price of an honest self-image, we are free of the need to draw our worth from another.
- When we pay the price of an intimate relationship with God, we are free to experience a truly significant relationship.
- When we pay the price of taking risks, we are free to emerge from behind walls we had hoped would keep us secure.
- When we pay the price of being honest about the possibility of pain, we are free to experience joy even in the midst of pain.
- When we pay the price of time, we are free from the tyranny of the superficial.
- When we pay the price of accountability, we are free from the need to second-guess or pretend. We are free to be honest.
- When we pay the price of perseverance, we are free to believe that God is determined to finish what He started.

As we pay these various prices, we will be free to experience a new understanding of God, of ourselves, and of relationships. As we gain this understanding, we will be free to enjoy intimacy.

Hear this important affirmation: the relationship is always bigger than the conflict.

CHAPTER TWELVE

Conflict: Who Needs It?

Several bumblebees were placed in a container empty of everything but stable air. The container functioned much like a space simulator: the air was free of obstacles and pressure. Interestingly, the bumblebees could not survive in this environment. Every one of them died despite what should have been an ideal, stress-free setting.

What conclusion did scientists draw from this discovery? A rather surprising one—and a rather surprising answer to the question that opens this chapter. The conclusion was that bumblebees cannot survive without stress—without obstacles. I maintain that we are like bumblebees in that respect. For us, too, obstacles are important in life. In fact, as I said in an earlier chapter, obstacles *are* life. Who, then, needs conflict? Every single one of us does!

Before you close this book in frustration or disbelief, let me explain something about conflict. First, consider David Augsburger's definition of conflict: "Conflict is natural, normal, neutral, and sometimes even delightful. It can turn into painful or disastrous ends, but it doesn't need to. Conflict is neither good nor bad, right nor wrong. Conflict simply is."[1] What is significant about conflict, then, is what we do with it. How we handle conflict is the issue here.

Basically, a conflict is a disagreement. And the disagreement can range from what color shirt to wear, to a political disagreement with a neighbor, to a misunderstanding with a friend, to receiving three different sides of a story from three different people, to feeling hurt by a friend or spouse, to a volatile discussion in which you find yourself in the role of antagonist—with many situations in between.

We all assume, however, that conflict is negative, and we all tend to play games with the word "conflict." Consider the phrase "the Korean conflict." The conflict was the misunderstanding about boundaries; the war was the way we dealt with it. As with any misunderstanding or disagreement—as with any conflict—the way we deal with it is the real issue. And yet most of us are afraid of conflict. Let's look at some of the reasons why.

1. We misunderstand conflict.

We seem to have adopted the myth that conflict automatically engages us in war. In reality, war is only one way—and a very poor way at that—to deal with conflict. We'll explore better options in this chapter.

2. We think that conflict interrupts life.

This idea comes from the myth that life is to be comfortable. The logical extension of this premise is that a violation of comfort is a violation of life. Life, however, as I've already mentioned, is by definition the handling of obstacles and conflict. It is impossible that life could be otherwise because we live in the world as human pinballs. Whenever two pinballs touch, friction is inevitable.

3. We do not have the skills to handle conflict.

Without the skills to deal with a situation, we are understandably intimidated by it. A conflict is no different. We experience tension and stress when we don't know what to say or do in the face of a conflict.

Having acknowledged the two myths that conflict inevitably leads to war and that life was meant to be conflict-free, you can now move on to a healthy way of dealing with conflict. The rest of this chapter will help you develop skills in conflict resolution. And since obstacles are life (i.e., conflicts are life), these skills in conflict resolution are also skills in life management and relationship management.

As you have undoubtedly learned from experience, friction is part of relationships. Let me assure you that this friction is a *normal* part of relationships. (If there isn't that friction, one of you must be dead!) As a pastor, I teach people how to deal with this friction not so that they can once again find comfort but, more importantly, so that they can develop important skills for their journey called life. I want them to learn, for instance, how to deal with an occasional misunderstanding and how to talk to the person involved. This education can be valuable for each one of us. Here are some basic lessons.

• My identity is not defined by conflict.

As we've seen again and again throughout this book, a person in a state of dependence will be threatened when a conflict arises. If, for instance, my identity is tied to how the conflict is resolved, I stand to lose respect and friendship depending on the outcome of the situation. Furthermore, if my identity is tied to the conflict, I will enter any attempt at resolution with a hidden agenda: I will be wanting and needing to prove something, to get something, or to blame something or someone in order to preserve my identity as an okay person.

When I do not have this hidden agenda, I am free to seek resolution because I won't need to be right or wrong. The issue of right or wrong is only important if my identity is at stake. Only then do I regard conflict as a win-or-lose situation, and in that case I will be seeking vindication rather than resolution. Ironically, the other person will usually react by doing the same thing.

Also, if I have a hidden agenda, my creativity will be stifled. Problem solving will therefore be more difficult. My energy will be invested in this hidden agenda, and I will have no energy left for honesty, listening, or trying to understand.

As you can see, conflict can only be intensified when we feel that our very identity is threatened by the resolution of that conflict. Let go of that myth, and rest in the fact that your identity is in the hands of your loving God. Then you will be free to work through and grow through the resolution of any misunderstanding or disagreement you may be facing.

• Conflict is not an enemy to intimacy.

Hear this important affirmation: the relationship is always bigger than the conflict. Unfortunately, when we are in the midst of dealing with a conflict, we tend to become myopic. We assume that the entire relationship will be summed up or defined by or consumed by the way we handle this one conflict. In other words, we assume that the outcome of one conflict will be the outcome of the relationship itself. We need to step back and see the bigger picture, though. The commitment we have made in the relationship—the commitment we have made to the other person—provides a bigger foundation than any conflict can destroy. Remind yourself of this fact. Tell yourself again and again that a conflict is not bigger than your identity, that it is not bigger than your relationship, and that you are therefore free. You don't need to be a victim of any conflict!

• **Conflict is not resolved serendipitously.**

Conflict is not resolved by luck or happenstance. Conflict is resolved by skills and management. Conflict is a management problem rather than merely a time problem. Sleeping on it is fine because that act can give a person a new perspective. The distance can offer management space. Sleeping on it is not designed, however, to make the conflict magically disappear. Magic doesn't work; management does—and with practice we get better at managing the conflicts in our life.

We can only practice, though, when we understand what we are facing. I have noticed three types of conflict, each of which is resolved differently. First let me list the three types of conflict:

1. Hurt: I've been violated.
2. Unmet Expectations: I've been disappointed.
3. Confrontation: I need to confront you, my friend, about an unhealthy lifestyle.

Now let's consider how to deal sensitively and effectively with each situation.

Hurt

1. Be honest about the source of the hurt.

A lot of people are oversensitive—are you one of them? Some people too readily play the role of victim or martyr—are you doing just that in this situation? Ask yourself ultimately, "Is this a legitimate hurt that I am feeling?"

2. Remind yourself that your identity is not defined by that hurt.

If my identity is defined by a hurt, I'll forever be the victim of that hurt. I will forever need the person who hurt me to

149

release me from this wounded state. Only then will I be okay. In the meantime, I am immobilized. I can only wait for whatever freeing actions or words that person may offer me—and that wait will more than likely be indefinite. You don't need to fall into that trap. You don't need to be like my friend Marge. For twenty-five years she had nursed the hurt that came from the fact that her mother never apologized to her for abusive things she did during Marge's childhood. Her mother died, still without apologizing to her daughter, and Marge had imprisoned herself as a victim of these hurts and this lack of apology.

3. Practice forgiveness.

You can do the releasing. You can free yourself from the hurt. You are in the position to give up the right to hurt the person who first hurt you. This forgiveness will set you free. You will be able to move forward.

These three steps of dealing with hurt allow us to be honest about the hurt we're feeling without going to unhealthy extremes. A victim, for instance, gives the hurt too much power while a repressor denies the hurt. Step #1—being honest about the hurt—overcomes the repressor's tendency to deny. Step #2—understanding that your identity is not at stake—overcomes the tendency to be victimized by the situation. Together, Steps #1 and #2 allow you to take Step #3. Remember that the step of forgiveness is a choice, a conscious decision of the will, rather than an emotion that you must wait to descend upon you.

Let me also mention that it is not necessarily true that you need to go to the person and extend your forgiveness. That is okay to do if you are sure that the exchange will be a healthy one and if you are sure that your motives are pure and loving. Forgiveness, however, takes place within you. The other person's response cannot validate or invalidate the forgiveness process.

150

Unmet Expectations

1. Declare your expectations to yourself.

I think of one husband I spoke with. He explained that he was feeling hurt. When I asked him why he was feeling hurt, he explained that he didn't think that his wife had enough class in public. I worked with him to help him see that he wasn't hurt; he was instead dealing with unmet expectations. Forgiving his wife for not having class would not—could not—be the answer. He needed to deal with his unmet expectations, and that involves different steps than dealing with hurt.

First, he, like all of us, needs to be honest about his expectations. He needs to write down his specific ideas and hopes about what the other person should do. While a person may not think that he or she has a set of expectations, I maintain that these expectations always come out in conflict. Each one of us will become aware of our expectations when we are suddenly bothered by something. Perhaps we had repressed these expectations; perhaps we had not even thought about what our expectations were. Having realized a certain expectation, we now need to determine whether it is legitimate.

2. Check the motive behind your expectation.

Jesus warned us about expectations and evaluations of other people. He asked the penetrating question, "Why do you look at the speck of sawdust in your brother's eye and pay no attention to the plank in your own eye?" (Matthew 7:3) When you consider your expectations for another person, you must first consider whether the issue may not be your problem. The man I just mentioned may have to come to terms with the fact that the real problem is not that his wife isn't classy.

151

The problem may instead be his own feelings about himself or some pent-up anger about something she said or did.

Another important reading to take when you're evaluating your expectations is whether your identity is intact. Ask yourself, "Am I being owned by these expectations of you? Do I take unmet expectations personally? Do I feel like you're abusing me when you let me down?" Let me add that it is quite likely that the person is completely unaware of your expectations for him or her—and that hardly makes the situation an abusive one!

Checking the motives behind your expectations boils down, once again, to the question, "Who or what owns me? The plank in my eye? My unstable identity?" Answer these questions before moving on to the next step.

3. Based on your motivation, determine whether this situation requires confrontation.

Ask yourself, "What will be accomplished if I confront this person? What purpose will be served? Will the confrontation be healthy for the relationship? (Is it, for example, important for me to let you know that you aren't very classy in public?) Is the confrontation in your best interest? Is it in the best interest of the relationship? Do I have a hidden agenda?" These questions require honest answers. Once you have arrived at the decision to confront the person, you can move to the next step.

4. If the situation is worth discussing, go to the person involved—not to a third party.

It isn't right or fair or loving to tell everyone in the world that your wife is not classy in public—and then fail to tell her. Everyone knows except the person who needs to know—and those other people shouldn't know in the first place!

Go, therefore, to the person involved. First establish an environment of trust. That trust can only happen if you approach the person without any kind of hidden agenda. That person will see that you don't have any ulterior motives and will know that you are there in the best interest of the relationship.

Once you have discussed the situation with the person, allow room for growth. Allow time for change. Demanding change overnight is unrealistic; demanding change overnight is an action right off a hidden agenda you are holding.

Finally, when you approach the person, be ready and willing to help him or her pursue creative alternatives. Don't back the person into a corner. That person will have no choice but to come out fighting. Instead, be willing to stand with the person and to work together to improve the situation.

Unhealthy Lifestyle

1. Check the motive behind your desire to confront the person.

As we looked at in the guidelines for dealing with unmet expectations, the step of looking honestly at your motivation is important. What, if anything, is on your hidden agenda? Are you, for instance, trying to prove yourself more spiritual than the person you are confronting? Is there a plank in your eye which should be the focus of your energy instead of the speck in your brother's or sister's eye?

2. Reaffirm your love for the person by praying for him or her.

I can't emphasize enough that only someone willing to pray for a person has the right to confront that person about his or her lifestyle. That person's situation could, but for the grace

153

of God, be yours. Therefore, turn to God for His guidance and wisdom in how you should deal with the situation: "God, You created my friend for abundant life. How can I now be a part of a loving confrontation that will help that person realize Your love and Your will for his/her actions? Please be with me, God. Show me the way You would have me deal with this situation in love."

3. Go directly to the person, not to a third party.

How many times have you heard this kind of prayer request? "I would like all of you to pray for poor Jane. She is only fourteen years old and she is pregnant. She really needs our prayers because of her boyfriend's pressure to get an abortion. Her folks are not being too supportive, either. The whole situation is unfair and tragic. When will kids these days learn? They continue to mess up their lives. Anyway, please pray for young, pregnant Jane."

This kind of prayer request is nothing more than gossip. And this kind of gossip is inappropriate and wrong. Gossip veiled in terms of a prayer request or a tirade against the latest social sin is still gossip. Third parties do not need to know details in order to pray for situations which you are concerned about. When prayer requests are shared, be sure once again that your motives are pure—that you are not using your knowledge of a situation as a status symbol or as an attention getter.

4. Express your concern in a positive way.

Verbally affirm that your intentions are loving and are for that person's own good. Approach your friend in love and in genuine humility. Any sense of judgment or superiority will serve only to negate the good you are trying to accomplish. Simply put, if you feel superior when you are confronting the person, you are in the wrong.

If the person responds to you by attacking, put that reaction in perspective. Never take the attack personally. It is always more reflective of the individual doing the attacking than it is of the person being attacked. The attack reveals that a nerve was touched—it reveals the presence of a wound. The attack has no bearing on the person attacked. Do not, therefore, be deterred by a violent and perhaps hurtful reaction.

Allow room for growth when you do confront the person. Expect the best; expect improvement. Pray for that growth, and pray for guidance as to how you may be able to facilitate it. Ask God to show you how to be a friend in this situation. This may seem like an odd statement to make, but consider how often we are surprised when Jane does come through the difficult situation. Our surprise at her decision to have the child and give it up for adoption is indicative of our skepticism that our prayers will be answered. Our surprise reveals our failure to expect improvement and growth.

Although we have looked at three types of conflict and constructive steps to take in dealing with each kind, the best guideline for dealing with conflict is to understand its inevitability. Conflict *is* inevitable. Understand, too, that agreeing to disagree is not a bad thing. It is, in fact, a very healthy thing that allows us to share ourselves and our ideas. Agreeing to disagree is a significant building block for intimacy.

Remember, too, that conflict need not be a threat to your identity. If someone doesn't agree with me, that different opinion or way of thinking is not a threat to my identity. Once I accept that fact—once I allow that person to be different from me—then I'm free to respond: I'm free to be honest, assertive, open, straightforward, affirming, and encouraging.

155

Conflict, therefore, does not need to mean war. You can throw down your weapons. You can turn them into plowshares and cultivate the ground for loving and open interaction.

If you or I see intimacy as something we suddenly have and will have for life—if we see intimacy as the finish line in a race we're running—we see intimacy wrongly.

CHAPTER THIRTEEN

Where Do I Go from Here? Steps to an Intimate Lifestyle

The advertisement couldn't help but catch my attention. Covering a full-page in a well-known national magazine, it offered a book and set of tapes. The bold-faced headline for the "Connecting System" read "How to Get the Love You Never Thought You Could" and the copy that followed made some interesting claims: "A system so good, so effective, so foolproof, that the publishers are willing to GUARANTEE that you will find love. . . . Why spend another day of your life lonely and without love? . . . Don't cheat yourself of the greatest emotion men and women experience together. Order the 'Connecting System' today and discover how easy it is to get the love you always wanted but never thought you could."

This fantastic breakthrough was available for only $23.90 plus $2.00 shipping. The ad I saw also offered "the amazing best-seller that shows you how to start a conversation with *anyone, anywhere*." The book *100 Best Opening Lines* would be included if I ordered the "Connecting System" today.

I laughed—but *they* got rich!

And they got rich by catering to one of our biggest desires—our desire for intimacy. Technique would be taught and success guaranteed for less than thirty dollars. That's a small price for such a prize! Perhaps we could sell this book for that price! Unfortunately, though, *we* are fresh out of guarantees. I am not, however, out of practical suggestions about where we go from here. We can take specific steps to reinforce and to practice what we have learned. We can live out the truths that we have discovered.

Step #1: Join with Fellow Journeyers

We need to take seriously what we learned in the earlier chapters: growth happens in the context of community. We were made to be in relationship with God and with one another, and when we are in these relationships, we grow. Put simply, *I* grow as *we* grow. It would therefore be a fatal mistake to begin to take these steps toward intimacy with the assumption that I am capable of taking them all on my own.

Furthermore, we may even be confused about what steps to take. Many of us tend to read books such as this one and turn the ideas discussed into a set of rules. We then compound this error by vowing to ourselves to follow all the "rules" to the letter. It doesn't take long before we fail, though, and the consequences are sometimes devastating. There can be, for instance, intense guilt because we thought we "had what it took" to succeed. Having let ourselves down, we now assume that we no longer measure up to the standards of those around us. It's as if we have destined ourselves to a path of performance, guilt, and self-chastisement. We can, however, move from this way of thinking when we turn to God.

Consider that Christian faith is built on the foundation that God became a man: He became a part of the human race in the person Jesus Christ. The gospel of John explains: "The Word became flesh and lived for a while among us" (John 1:14). While this is a unifying fact for Christians, it is necessary to affirm that the Incarnation occurred for more than mere solidarity. The Incarnation and resulting community provide us a place of healing and refuge. Jesus, having lived on this earth, can understand what we are going through. As the writer of Hebrews explains, we never need to feel that no one understands us: "For we do not have a high priest who is unable to sympathize with our weaknesses, but we have one who has been tempted in every way, just as we are—yet was without sin. Let us then approach the throne of grace with confidence, so that we may receive mercy and find grace to help us in our time of need" (Hebrews 4:15-16).

As One who can "sympathize with our weaknesses," Jesus gives us a new understanding of what it means to stand alongside another person. Because He came to stand alongside us, we are now able to stand alongside one another. We are free to see each other as fellow journeyers—not as competitors, judges, or enemies. We are free to share with each other any lessons we learn. We are free to experience a new type of community.

Do not assume, therefore, that you can carry your own load. Do not become burdened by the pressure to prove yourself by trying to walk alone. Welcome to the human race! Join with us and others as we journey together—as we discover the joys and sorrows, the gladness and pain of what it means to be fully alive.

Step #2: Discard Your Myths about Intimacy

On the basis of Step #1, we will assume that Steps #2-#9 do not have to be carried out in isolation. We can help one another by sharing the load. Now, as we have said before, the first step of growth is honesty. Until I am honest about where I am, I will not be able to move on. Until I can confess—take responsibility for who I am and where I am—I will not be able to grow.

In light of this truth, we need to look honestly at the myths about intimacy which we carry with us into our relationships. These myths only serve to confuse us and to hinder our attempts to share ourselves. What, then, are the myths that you continue to carry? What are the myths that you wish to discard? Consider some of these very popular—and very false!—ideas:

- Intimacy always expresses itself sexually.
- Intimacy is possible only with the opposite sex.
- Intimacy is possible only within marriage.
- Intimacy is easy.
- Intimacy is built on such externals as physical appearance.
- Intimacy is an emotion.
- Intimacy is exempt from pain and is threatened by conflict.

If I am afraid to tell you about the myths and fears I am struggling with, then I am destined to stay where I am—stuck in the midst of them. We are, however, free to discard our myths. We do this by simply confessing—by honestly acknowledging—where we are and which myths we are carrying with us. Still, such honesty is a risk on the journey toward intimacy—and I am often afraid of such a risk. Somehow I have been convinced that I need to hide the fact that I have not yet "arrived." By confessing my myths, though, I am admitting to you and to myself that I am still a fellow jour-neyer, a fellow struggler.

At this point, I need to be reminded again that my identity is not tied to my need to perform for you. I don't need to try to prove to you that I am someone I am not. With this step of confession, then, I am free to grow. With this step, I am free to move on. Having acknowledged a myth, I am free to say that it is inappropriate and wrong, and therefore I am free to discard it.

You, too, can be free of myths and free to grow. A step of confession is all it takes, and here is an opportunity: "I confess that I have believed the myth that says _____ . I now affirm that this myth is untrue and that it need not have power over my identity. I am free to move on."

Step #3: Let Go of the Past

Because we live in a broken world, we all know, to one degree or another, what it's like to be a casualty in the struggle for intimacy. We understand rejection, hurt, disappointment, hopelessness, fear, and pain. We all carry with us scars and bruises from events in our life. We carry memories of failures, reminders of past hurts, and various other emotional baggage which only serve to cripple us and our efforts toward intimacy. All of us, therefore, need to be healed.

Do you remember the John 5 account of Jesus healing the man at the pool of Bethesda? This person had been an invalid for thirty-eight years and yet the first thing that Jesus said to him was, "Do you want to be healed?" While at first glance this question may seem callous and insensitive, it emphasizes a fundamental truth about human nature. The presence of sickness does not guarantee a desire for health. Likewise, the presence of emotional baggage does not guarantee the desire for wholeness.

Still, we need healing. We need to be set free from the self-imposed prison of our past. If we have failed in a particular area or if we have been rejected or hurt, our tendency is to hang on to that failure or pain or hurt to the point that it becomes our identity. We then find ourselves relating to people according to that identity.

This frame of mind keeps me very self-centered. John Powell observes, "This is a pain-filled world, and so, a loveless world that we live in. Most human beings are so turned-in by their own pains that they cannot get enough out of themselves to love to any great extent."[1] John Powell is right. A person can't find love when his or her focus is entirely inward. Neither can a person find relationship or intimacy. Preoccupation with self moves us to protect rather than share ourselves. We want to remain secure, comfortable, and safe—and soon we find ourselves in secure, self-imposed prisons. To avoid love and intimacy, then, you need only to stay focused on yourself.

Making this situation worse is the fact that my preoccupation with myself often masquerades as nobility. I make my self-pity, fear of rejection, pain from loss, or need for fairness a noble venture. How? By receiving strokes for my self-pity—and I interpret these strokes as love. This "love" does not force me to reach out and care, and there is no need for risk. I get the attention I want when I hear from you, "Poor dear! You really are going through difficult times." While your words may make me feel somewhat noble, they also serve to keep me safe behind my walls of self-pity.

Perhaps it is now easier to see how self-imposed prisons arise from a focus on self—and such a focus does not allow love. To love—to be intimate—I must step out of myself and away from my concerns. To love, I must learn the art of giving up. Giving up can begin with our willingness to be healed: we will experience healing when we let go of—or give up—certain things from the past. Does this mean that we deny the pain and hurt from the past? Do we pretend that they did not exist? No. We do not deny the reality of pain or failure or hurt, but neither do we allow this reality to control our identity or our future. Our pain, our past failures, our unhealed hurt, and our unnecessary emotional baggage do not have to tell us who we are.

Let me repeat this. To love, I must learn the art of giving up. Giving up is possible because healing is possible, and the two go together. Healing gives us a true and proper perspective of our identity. Giving up is recognizing that certain things do not have the power to tell me who I am. Consider some things you might have to give up as you learn to love:

- To receive your love, I must give up my expectation that you will not find me worthy of love.
- To receive your love, I must give up my need to see my life as a replay of past hurts.
- To receive your love, I must give up my need to prove to you and everyone else that I am okay.

- To receive your love, I must give up my need to see life as fair.
- To receive your love, I must give up my need to possess you, as if you could "make me ok."

Such giving up is not easy because it isn't done one time— once and for all. That which we attempt to give up continues to return as if it were on a rubber band. Giving up our self-pity, our walls of protection, and the unhealthy basis of our identity is possible only after we have heard and received the words of healing. For the painful memories, disappointments, and broken dreams are not merely "discarded," but are replaced by a healthy understanding of "who owns us."

What emotional baggage we may ask? Think about the following questions: What keeps you from giving of yourself? What keeps you from reaching out to people and caring about them? What keeps you from taking risks? What keeps you from entering into life's moments for fear of disappointment?

This giving up can help us take the important step of letting go of our past and our unhealthy tendency to let it control us. This step, though, runs counter to our natural tendency to enjoy the comfort of the familiar—even when that familiar is a collection of trinkets or emotional baggage of pain and hurt from the past. We will be moving toward freedom and toward healing when we let Jesus take from us the burden of our past.

Step #4: Focus on Intimate Behavior

You may be a lot like me. I want to be able to simply read a book or attend a seminar or listen to a lecture and then be able to say with confidence, "Hello, there. My name is Terry—and I am intimate." If you or I see intimacy as something we suddenly have and will have for life—if we see intimacy as the finish line in a race we're running—we see intimacy wrongly. If we see intimacy as a place where we will eventually arrive, we are destined to frustration. When we focus on intimacy as a final destination, we cease to focus on love. We instead focus on security. Security seeks guarantees. Security asks for a place where we can enjoy benefits without being called on to give or to risk or to care.

In our growth towards intimacy, our emphasis must not be on intimacy as a place where we have arrived, but instead on *intimacy as the outcome of intimate behavior.* I cannot instantly achieve intimacy in a relationship. I cannot be sure that intimacy will be part of a relationship I enter. I can, however, take responsibility for intimate behavior. Let me suggest some different words and actions which encourage openness and sharing in a relationship:

- Say "thank you"
- Offer words of appreciation
- Compliment the one you care about
- Let him/her cry
- Let yourself cry in front of him/her
- Show your weakness
- Say "I love you" even if you're sure he/she knows it anyway
- Listen to an opinion even when you know you're going to disagree
- Confess a fault or mistake

Rather than being an emotion which mysteriously descends upon us, intimacy is—as this list suggests—something dynamic and alive that we need to nurture. Intimacy is always growing and changing as we work with the building blocks called "intimate behaviors." When I focus my attention on these behaviors rather than on intimacy as some general concept, then I begin to take responsibility for today. I am no longer anxiously yet passively waiting for intimacy to happen to me. The guiding question in my growth changes from "When will I experience intimacy?" to "What intimate behaviors am I willing to risk doing today?" This new way of thinking helps intimacy become more tangible for us. Intimacy is no longer out there somewhere. Nor is it only for the relational elite. Intimacy becomes something we construct with small, manageable building blocks.

As Step #4 suggests, intimacy happens with little steps. Intimacy is possible because of small, understandable choices I make to behave in certain ways. In our desire for the immediate, the big, the elaborate, and the ecstatic, we may miss small, quiet, and very intimate words and actions. As I mentioned before, Paul Tournier once observed that "Many people spend their entire life indefinitely preparing to live."[2] Likewise, many people spend their entire life indefinitely preparing to be intimate. The steps in this chapter and in the next can help you be a person who experiences intimacy rather than one who just waits for it.

Intimacy must start slowly. It's all right if the initial building blocks are small. Just be sure that they are solid: be sure that you are actually revealing who you really are.

CHAPTER FOURTEEN

Where Do I Go from Here?
The Journey Continues

Joan knew the meaning of hope. She was a fighter and an optimist. She was always there to support the underdog. Lesser persons would have given up long before—but not Joan! She was convinced that God really meant it when He said He would give her an abundant life. Life, though, had not always been easy for Joan. I suppose there was an irony to her strong sense of hope.

Joan had known tough times. She was a woman in her fifties. When I met her, she was now single again after being married twice. Both marriages had ended in divorce, one by her choice—she was a victim of abuse—and the other by the choice of her spouse. At one time, she seriously doubted her ability to provide the kind of love that sustains a marriage.

Joan had a daughter in her mid-twenties. Joan described their relationship as "quite rocky and fragile." Her daughter resented her for the two divorces and had told her on more than one occasion that she "hated" her.

Joan lived with and took care of her mother, a deaf woman who was, for all practical purposes, an invalid. Joan worked a secretarial job to make ends meet and, because of her relationship with her mother, had very little time for a social life.

When Joan told her story, tears would come to her eyes, but they were not tears of defeat. They were tears that reflected her experiences of pain. Behind Joan's tears were a sense of victory, an attitude of joy, and a confidence based on hope in Jesus Christ.

Joan could have easily played the game of "If only . . ."; she could have merely waited for her ship to come in and take her away from her problems. But she didn't. She could have become bitter and resentful. But she didn't. She could have given up on life and settled for the mediocre. But she didn't. Joan didn't quit and she didn't complain. Instead, she saw obstacles in life as opportunities for growth.

You may be wondering why I'm talking about Joan in a book about intimacy. The reason is this: she was one of my greatest teachers. She defied the stereotype of an intimate person. She was not married or dating. She was not a swinger and she had no opportunities to date. Her commitment to her mother and her own appearance were obstacles to dating relationships. She was not one of the "beautiful people"— until she smiled.

Joan had learned to accept life as a gift. Although she had learned vulnerability and honesty the hard way, she moved forward. She built an intimacy with God, her mother, and herself that would be a good model for us all. She did not pretend about the obstacles in her life; she lived with them openly and honestly. She was free to give whatever she had, and what she had, she gave. She fully expressed herself to God, and she fully gave herself to her mother. She had no need to play games in relationships. She had no need to protect herself from others. From the outside, one might assume Joan to be a failure at intimacy. As I said, she wasn't one of the "beautiful people," but she lived a joyous and beautiful life.

This chapter is dedicated to the Joans of this world—to people who are willing to walk with their heads held high along this journey of life, this journey toward intimacy.

People who are willing to see obstacles as opportunities, not enemies. People who live with an underlying reservoir of hope. People who know that God never promised roses without thorns or rainbows without storms. People who know that intimacy is a journey and a gift, not a campground or a right.

I would like to have been able to paint for you a picture of an intimacy free of obstacles and defeat, but that picture would be both unfair and unreal. As we finish walking through these steps to an intimate lifestyle, we need to face life as it is, not life as we wish it would be. Then, as we move towards intimacy, we will be basing our hope not on fantasy but on a faithful God and a real understanding of the world in which we live.

Step #5: Learn from the Closure of Relationships

I have discovered that one of the enemies of intimacy is our inability to deal with the end of a relationship. When a relationship ends, we assume that we must discard everything and start from scratch in the next relationship. We assume that all is lost. We assume that we are destined to perpetual failure in relationships. These assumptions do not allow for the healthy closure of past relationships. Furthermore, this inability to deal with closure not only becomes a self-fulfilling prophecy for future relationships, but it also robs us of the possibility of learning from our past, from our pain, from our hurt, and from our mistakes.

Not all closure, though, is the same. Some of my relationships have ended because of my choice; others have ended against my choice. While these situations are very different from each other, we can learn from both. Let's look at each case individually.

Closure by Personal Choice

You are in a relationship that should end for one of a variety of reasons ranging from the very serious (abuse) to the not-so-serious ("I'm just too busy right now"). When do you close this relationship? And how do you learn from that closure? All relationships are not created equal—each has its unique aspects—but there are some general principles which apply.

(a) I must be willing to pay the price of honesty.

Many relationships end in the same way that they began—shrouded in mystery. Expectations were never mentioned, and level of commitment was never discussed. Often we have done this with the hope that if a firm verbal commitment is not made, the relationship will be easier to leave if "things don't work out." Chances are that if a relationship began with such hiding and lack of openness, its ending may be handled in just as dishonest and unfair a manner.

However the relationship began, though, honesty is fundamental in closure. In the same way that I should choose to be completely up-front with regard to my expectations and commitments at the beginning of a relationship, so also must I be willing to be honest at the close. Very often, though, we will avoid honesty—even with ourselves. Instead of giving the real reason for wanting to end or redefine a relationship, we find ourselves concocting various stories, all in an attempt to avoid peeling back a corner of that protective personage. The fact remains that honesty is necessary for the healthy closure or redefinition of a relationship.

(b) I must be willing to pay the price of accountability.

In the same way that I must be honest with you about my emotions, I must also be honest about the issue of our commitment. Accountability says that commitments are made—consciously or subconsciously—and must be taken seriously. I need to be honest about the forces working against the relationship; I need to be honest about my feelings. I must say to you directly, "This is not a relationship I choose to be in right now" or "This relationship is not healthy for me." I must be willing then to answer your questions honestly and sensitively.

Closure by the Other Person

All of us have probably experienced the closure of a relationship against our will. In a divorce, for instance, parents often leave children. In other situations, friends become acquaintances; boyfriends or girlfriends decide that they would rather be "just friends"; husbands and wives walk away from their marriage. Relationships end—not necessarily for good reasons and not necessarily by our choice—but some relationships do end. Can we learn from this kind of closure?

(a) Avoid seeing yourself as the victim.

You may have had little or nothing to do with the end of the relationship. It may have been "completely the other person's fault." Even so, if you assume the role of being the victim, you forfeit responsibility for your life, for your choices, and for your growth. By choosing to be a victim you say, "I will wait for life to be done unto me. I am unable to take responsibility for myself, so I reluctantly hand it over to you."

You and I may have had no choice in the closure of a relationship, but we do have choices and responsibility when it comes time to respond to that closure. By being a "victim," though, I sentence myself to the prison of a puppet's life. I spend my days fantasizing about the day that someone will come into my life and "make me somebody." As a victim,

I play games which begin with the sentence "If only . . ." as I try to convince myself that I wouldn't be in this mess if only my circumstances were different.

(b) Learn to forgive.

If the relationship has ended against your will, it is probably fair to say that you are experiencing legitimate hurt. Forgiveness does not deny that this hurt exists; forgivenness does not deny reality. In fact, forgiveness recognizes and affirms the reality of the hurt. Without the presence of the hurt, there would be nothing to forgive! Forgiveness, however, is not the same as forgetting. If I have forgotten the incident, there is nothing to forgive. I myself, though, have spent much of my life feeling guilty because of my inability to forget. I have believed that because I hadn't forgotten, I hadn't forgiven. Forgetting, though, is the amputation method of healing. We hope that by cutting off our arm we can get rid of the pain in our hand, but in actuality the pain only moves.

Also, as we all know, forgiveness is difficult. It is always easier to blame. I want everyone, including God, to see how and where I was wronged: "After all, he said he would call, and he didn't"; "She told me I was the 'only one', but now I know I'm not"; or "Dad said he was going to take me on a trip—but he didn't have time." We feel hurt and so we feel that we deserve some kind of revenge or at least some special compensation. This need for fairness or revenge only serves to keep me tied to the person who hurt me and to the past. I will soon discover, too, that no amount of dwelling on the past or fantasizing about revenge will even the score.

To forgive is to set myself free—and I can choose to do this. Let me add that since forgiveness *is* a choice, a person acting the victim will be unable to forgive. A victim plays a passive role in life. A person who extends forgiveness must take the active role of making the decision and acting on it—a role quite different from that of the victimized and wounded person. In an act of forgiveness, I choose to say to the person who hurt me: "I give up my right to hurt you back, to seek revenge, to get even, and to make things fair."

Forgiveness therefore sets me free: I am free from my need to settle the score, to prove my innocence, or to convince people how wrong the other person was. In forgiveness, I choose (there's that word again) not to be owned by that person. I choose to be owned by God: I give my identity back to Him.

Since forgiveness is a choice, forgiveness is not to be governed by my emotions. My emotions may completely contradict my choice to forgive. That's okay. That does not mean that the act of forgiveness is invalid. In fact, we would rarely—if ever—be able to forgive if the act of forgiveness were dependent on our feelings. In this life we lead, we never have stable feelings. We would therefore never be able to forgive a person. As I've said, though, an act of forgiveness is tied to our choice, not to our feelings. Let me also remind you that forgiveness can be slow. Like the process of intimacy, the process of forgiveness requires time, effort, and practice. You can, however, begin that process today with the decision to forgive the one who hurt you.

(c) Give up ownership.

Forgiveness is difficult because we want to maintain some sense of ownership of the former relationship. For whatever reasons, conscious or not, I want some connection to that person because I thought he/she existed for me. The irony of this ownership is that the thing or person that we think *we* own ends up owning us. It owns our time, our energy, our thoughts, and our worries.

I also see ownership as a form of pride that says, "I'm afraid to admit that I'm not in control here!" Because the relationship *affected* my identity as well as *reflected* it for a certain period of time, I feel the need to maintain some control. I am, therefore, afraid to give up the other person and whatever part of my identity might be involved. Surrendering ownership, however, is a step of closure that brings hope. It can help us face our unfulfilled expectations and the truth that life is sometimes not fair. When we learn these things, we will be able to share more of ourselves in another relationship—which brings me to the next step.

(d) Avoid isolation.

My temptation is to respond to a hurtful relationship by saying, "That's it! That's the last time I'll be vulnerable. That's the last time I'll give myself away so freely." I seriously consider withdrawing to my island fortress to begin building walls for myself.

People opt for these various forms of isolation because they feel that they wouldn't have much to offer if they were to enter into a relationship. Their self-esteem is low, they feel like failures, and so they want to avoid people. If you are in this situation now, listen to these words: the people you are avoiding need you as much as you need them. Isolating yourself hurts them and you because you both lose the opportunity to risk and to try, to live and to love. So leave your island. Come out from behind those walls. You have nothing at all to gain from isolating yourself.

Having looked at two kinds of closure and various ways of dealing with it, we now need to discard—once and for all—the myth that closure is always an enemy to my ability to be intimate again. To assume such is to create a situation where I will never risk again. In closure there is pain and there is loss, but that does not mean that hope is gone. That pain becomes a teacher from which we can learn and grow. Still, we can let ourselves play the victim and stay stuck in that role. We can let the one who hurt us define our identity—we have been rejected and we are failures—and stay stuck

178

there. We can isolate ourselves and stay stuck in our hurt. Or we can choose to forgive, and it is that choice which will move us forward.

Step #6: Don't Assume Responsibility for the Other Person's Acceptance or Rejection of You

When we take the risk of sharing ourselves with someone, we easily fall into the trap of assuming responsibility for that other person's acceptance or rejection of us: "If he/she accepts me, it is because of the way I performed"—so I must continue that performance in order to continue receiving that favorable response; "If he/she rejects me, it is because of my inability to perform"—so I must live with the idea that I am a failure and incompetent in relationships. The obvious difficulty with this is that we find ourselves immediately back in the dependence stage of relational development. (See chapter 5.) Ironically, that stage of dependence comes with a guarantee: stagnant and unhealthy relationships are inevitable.

Although none of us wants that kind of relationship, many of us still take responsibility for another person's acceptance or rejection of us. When I do that, then I have an excuse to hide my inner self from you and I'll have an automatic scapegoat to blame when I am rejected. If I'm taking responsibility for your reaction to me, I'll be guarding what I say. Our relationship will easily degenerate to game-playing as we fail to take the risk of sharing ourselves. Just as I don't have power over your response to me, you don't have power over my freedom to risk—unless I give you that power. You won't have that power as long as I don't take responsibility for your acceptance or rejection of me.

179

Step #7: Take One Hurdle at a Time

Intimacy is not the result of any magical fantasies. Upon finishing this book, you will not be able to turn to a friend and say with confidence, "There! Now I'm intimate!" Haunted by the myth that says obstacles are an enemy to intimacy, you may dream about the day when all the obstacles to relationships will be gone and you will be able to go about the business of being intimate, but this fantasy does not fit with the experience of real life. Scott Peck was right when he wrote the opening sentence of his book *The Road Less Traveled*: "Life is difficult."[1] Life is a series of hurdles. Life is not the absence of conflict, problems, and interruptions. Life *is* the conflict, problems, and interruptions. Learning intimacy involves clearing these hurdles and dealing with these problems. Intimacy is not progress toward an ultimate or carefully defined finish line for when you reach the finish line in this life, you will be put six feet underground!

We can't, therefore, think of intimacy as something we'll find somewhere down the road or around the next corner because each of us has been handed only one day—today! We can and will find intimacy as we live today because intimacy is born in the labor pains of the problems and conflicts we will come up against. Take one hurdle of life at a time, and you'll be surprised at the opportunities for intimacy that you will find.

Step #8: Let Intimacy Involve the Whole Person

First, let me briefly describe what the whole person looks like. I'll do this by defining eight types of intimacy, each of which reveals a different aspect of a person.

1. *Emotional intimacy* is the ability to open the door to my fortress and allow you to see a little bit of who I am. This kind of intimacy

begins as I am able to peel back the corner of my personage. It develops as I find myself inadvertently coming out with a statement which reveals a little bit of me. While I may have been very much afraid that you would not accept it, when you do I am encouraged to share more of myself.

2. *Conflict intimacy* comes when two people share the desire to face and struggle with differences in order to enhance their relationship. If I am involved in a situation where someone says, "Terry, we need to become close friends," the first thing that I want to deal with in that relationship is, "Are we going to be able to share conflict intimacy?" It is important to me that we have a mutual understanding that conflict will not be a barrier in our relationship. It is important to me that we take the healthy stand that we are free to disagree with one another.

3. *Intellectual intimacy* is a closeness of ideas. Intellectual intimacy comes with common values, shared ways of thinking, or similar perceptions of beauty.

4. *Recreational intimacy* is the freedom to have fun together. It is the freedom to play, the freedom to enjoy, and the freedom to laugh. It happens when the children within us experience the joys of playing. In any relationship, recreational intimacy is probably the first level to develop because it is less threatening—everyone wants to have fun!

5. *Work intimacy* is the ability to share career or professional interests and goals. Work intimacy comes when people appreciate each other's goals and seek to better understand those goals.

6. *Spiritual intimacy* is honesty about our souls. It is also the means by which we allow God to complete our relationship. Think of God as the third point—the top point—of a triangle: as two people in relationship to each other grow closer to God, they will grow closer to each other. This growth happens when two people are able to pray, study the Bible, and worship together. When we are at prayer, we are most vulnerable. The willingness to pray, therefore, is the willingness to be vulnerable and is therefore a step toward intimacy with God as well as with your friend or spouse.

The symbol of the triangle is also important in its illustration of the fact that we need a solid foundation in our relationships. God can give us that foundation. A soul is too fragile to survive without a solid base. God can be that solid base. Consider for a moment that if you and I are not free to play together, the child in us dies. Similarly, if we are not free to sing and pray together, our souls become stagnant rather than joyful and alive. It is the spiritual intimacy which we share that will be the place of residence for joy in my life. Spiritual intimacy is the basis for sharing our joy for living.

7. *Crisis intimacy* is the ability to cope with the inevitable hurdles and pain of the relationship. Without crisis intimacy, we are willing to give up a relationship in the face of pain. I remember vividly an experience that a close friend and I shared. I did something which translated as deep rejection of him. It was a very hurtful behavior—the kind that says, "Okay, Charlie, we'll just go our separate ways." It took the two of us six months to come to the place where we could finally confront the issue. We were able to, though, because we knew that God had given us the ability to be intimate in spite of the wall we had hit. In spite of the hell we had put each other through, we could still talk about it and care for each other.

All of us can deal with a crisis—even an intensely painful one. We can even become more intimate through that experience because, by definition, a crisis touches us on a deep emotional level. We won't be able to cover up the emotions we experience during a crisis, and it is those feelings which we will be dealing with. This discussion of hopes and fears is a significant act of intimacy.

8. *Physical or sexual intimacy* involves more than just genital relationships. We are talking about the whole spectrum of physical intimacy—the look, the touch, the hug, the physical communication, and the sexual intercourse. In its proper context, physical intimacy is a beautiful act of consummation for two individuals who have allowed each other to give themselves completely to one another. Out of its proper context, of course, this type of intimacy can threaten the creation of a whole and balanced relationship.

As this eight-part discussion clearly points out, the whole person is involved in a relationship of genuine intimacy. All eight types should be present, and all should be happening at once. I have not rank ordered the different types—I don't want to give you an excuse to work on one to the exclusion of another that is "less important." I don't want you to regard intimacy as a formula of any kind. Just as intimacy touches the whole person, intimacy touches the entire experience of life.

Step #9: Understand that Intimacy Is Aerobic—and Live that Way!

The first time I took an aerobics class, I was sure that God had not created it! It must have been of the devil because there was intense pain. Those people were doing incredible things with their bodies! The contortions were unbelievable—and I hoped that I didn't look as clumsy as I felt. The fact remains, though, that toning muscles is an aerobic process: it takes time, persistence, and practice. If I am going to achieve a certain level of aerobic conditioning, I am going to have to put up with the pain of the practice.

Just as aerobic exercisers build up their pace slowly and just as distance runners start by running short races rather than marathons, people on the road to intimacy need to start slowly. I can't, for instance, put this book down with the confident exclamation: "Hey! I'm intimate!" I have to realize that I will not spontaneously become intimate. That is a popular and dangerous myth, and I am saddened by people who believe it. Couples planning their marriage, for instance, often respond with blank stares to my question, "What are you doing to develop intimacy?" They assume that when they are married, they will have instantly arrived. They assume that they will naturally and easily be intimate with one another. These assumptions are completely untrue, and so the question remains—what are *you* doing to develop intimacy?

My challenge to you is that you begin to work toward being honest with God, with yourself, and with others for ten minutes a day. That's the goal. Intimacy must start slowly like this. It's all right if the initial building blocks are small. Just be sure that they are solid: be sure that you are actually revealing who you really are. Slow, small, solid. For ten minutes a day, be open to rejection. For ten minutes a day, be vulnerable with God, with yourself, and with others. Be willing to say, for instance, "God, this is where I am. This is the myth I am using. These are the games I am playing. This is the mask I am wearing." That statement will be a significant step. Fight off any voice that may say, "You have to have intimacy at once!" Like doing an entire aerobics workout or running a marathon, living a life of intimacy is something we work toward gradually with slow, small, and solid steps.

Intimacy is worth the journey.

Throughout the preceding fourteen chapters, we have looked at various steps we can take toward intimacy. As these steps suggest, *intimacy is not without its price*. I know personally the struggle to achieve intimacy which Morris West describes so well in *The Shoes of the Fisherman*:

> It costs so much to be a full human being that there are very few who have the enlightenment, or the courage, to pay the price. . . . One has to abandon altogether the search for security, and reach out to the risk of living with both arms. One has to embrace the world like a lover, and yet demand no easy return of love. One has to accept pain as a condition of existence. One has to court doubt and darkness as the cost of knowing. One needs a will stubborn in conflict, but apt always to the total acceptance of every consequence of living and dying.[1]

I return to these words again and again not despite the fact that they are unsettling, but because they are unsettling. I need that.

And I guess that is one of the reasons I wanted to write this book: I wanted to get myself as well as my readers stirred up about this thing called "intimacy." I want to have more than a predictable life with a merely comfortable marriage. I want to learn how to give myself completely, how to receive love, and how to encourage an open environment of sharing and nurturing with Norva, my friend and my wife. And I want to be reminded that any warning about the cost of intimacy is small in comparison to the hope and fulfillment that await the willing journeyer. Intimacy *is* worth the journey: intimacy *is* worth the cost. Hear the words of Eugene Peterson, a fellow journeyer on the road to intimacy:

> Intimacy is no easy achievement. There is pain—longing, disappointment, and hurt. But if the costs are considerable, the rewards are magnificent, for in relationship with another and with the God who loves us we complete the humanity for which we were created. We stutter and stumble, wander and digress, delay and procrastinate; but we do learn to love even as we are loved, steadily and eternally, in Jesus Christ.[2]

Take with you on your own journey toward intimacy these words of hope and encouragement.

As you do travel this journey, you will—like me and everyone else—be carrying with you a lot of unnecessary baggage. In time, however, we can all learn the skills and gain the strength and confidence we need to let go of that baggage. We will also find that life is not waiting for us around the next corner. Instead, life is staring us in the face. It is what is happening now. In our fear and undue concentration on our baggage, we often miss opportunities to reap the very rewards that we've worked so hard to gain.

Consider this tale about a man traveling on trains in a country where the owners of the trains took no responsibility for personal items that were lost or stolen. To make matters worse, the man found himself on a train infamous for its history of personal burglaries, and the train ride was to be an overnighter. Worried about his luggage, the man found himself lying in bed and unable to sleep. His eyes were riveted to his luggage. The hours passed slowly until the clock showed 5:30 a.m. The man hadn't slept a wink when the inevitable happened—he drifted off. After a ten-minute doze, he woke with a start to find—you guessed it!—his luggage missing. His response? "Thank God! Now I can sleep!"

The message is simple: sometimes we are so wrapped up in potential obstacles that we fail to enjoy the journey. At other times we see the goal as unattainable and therefore we fail to recognize that we have begun the journey to that very goal.

Let me now share with you one of my favorite illustrations and encouragements about where the journey can lead. Listen to part of the discussion in the nursery which Margery Williams describes in her classic story *The Velveteen Rabbit*. The Rabbit has been puzzling over the concept of what is real. His companion explains:

> "It doesn't happen all at once," said the Skin Horse. "You become. It takes a long time. That's why it doesn't often happen to people who break easily, or have sharp edges, or who have to be carefully kept. Generally, by the time you are Real, most of your hair has been loved off, and your eyes drop out and you get loose in the joints and very shabby. But these things don't matter at all, because once you are Real you can't be ugly, except to people who don't understand."[3]

And let me add that once you are real you can't go back to being unreal!

Where, though, do we begin on the journey West outlines that leads to the rewards Williams describes? We begin with a commitment to the journey. If you do not believe that you have yet begun the journey toward intimacy, let this book be Step #1. If you are like me and have had glimpses of intimacy, let this book be an encouragement to you. In either instance, our focus can be summed up in this prayer: "God, sometimes we are afraid to commit ourselves and our lives to You. We are afraid to be known by You. Even though we are afraid, we would like to commit as much of ourselves to You as we can. We would like to commit as much of our lives to You as we can. God, I would like to give You permission to teach me about You and to lead me into an honest, game-free kind of intimacy with You, with myself, and with others. I choose, with your help and blessing, to embrace life in its fullness. Amen."

Let me close with this reminder: *intimacy is worth the journey*! If you are in a marriage or another type of significant relationship and are wondering whether intimacy is even possible when emotions wax and wane, when the "first love" is diminished, when it's easier to avoid an issue than to talk it through, then you need to hear that *intimacy is worth the journey*. If you are facing life as a single person and are wondering whether intimacy is possible in light of previous broken relationships, when it seems that the risks involved in building a relationship are too great, when you seriously question your own self-worth, when you wonder what you have to give someone else, then you need to hear that *intimacy is worth the journey*. Once the commitment to the journey is made, intimacy comes alive. Be glad that you are taking risks and trying to share yourself. Don't let the mountaintop goal of intimacy that you see ahead make you fail to see how far you've already come. Be thankful for the steps you've taken, and be glad that you aren't settling for less than the fulfillment that comes with truly intimate relationships.

Notes

Notes

CHAPTER 1

1. Tim Hansel in a lecture.

CHAPTER 2

1. Tim Hansel, *When I Relax I Feel Guilty* (Elgin, Illinois: David C. Cook Publishing Company, 1979), 80.

CHAPTER 3

1. Eric Berne in a lecture.
2. Keith Miller and Andrea Wells Miller, *The Single Experience* (Waco, Texas: Word Books, 1981), 20.
3. M. Scott Peck, *The Road Less Traveled* (New York: Touchstone, 1978), 81.
4. Keith Miller and Andrea Wells Miller, 20.
5. Keith Miller discusses this point on page 21.

CHAPTER 4

1. I am indebted to Paul Tournier for this discussion of persons and personages. He explains this concept in chapter 1 of *The Meaning of Persons*.
2. Alice Miller, *The Drama of the Gifted Child*, trans. Ruth Ward (New York: Basic Books, Inc., 1981), 25.
3. Paul Tournier, *The Meaning of Persons* (New York: Harper and Row, 1957), 9.
4. Ibid., 12.
5. Alice Miller, 15.

CHAPTER 5

1. Alice Miller, 17.
2. Tournier, 13.
3. Robert Merkle in a lecture.

CHAPTER 6

1. I was first introduced to the terms "hide and hurl" in J. Grant Howard, Jr.'s "Interpersonal Communication: Biblical Insights on the Problem and the Solution" (Portland, Oregon: Western Baptist Press, 1976), 6-7.
2. Tournier, 29.

CHAPTER 7

1. Bruce Larson in a lecture about other people telling us who we are.
2. Eugene H. Peterson, *A Long Obedience in the Same Direction* (Downers Grove, Illinois: InterVarsity Press, 1980), 61.

CHAPTER 8

1. Eugene H. Peterson, *Five Smooth Stones for Pastoral Work* (Atlanta: John Knox Press, 1980), 27.
2. Henri J. M. Nouwen, *Making All Things New: An Invitation to the Spiritual Life* (San Francisco: Harper and Row, 1981), 57.

CHAPTER 9

1. Peter Marin, "A Revolution's Broken Promises," *Psychology Today* (July 1983): 52.
2. Mel White, *The Other Side of Love* (Old Tappan, New Jersey: Fleming H. Revell Company, 1978), 18-19.
3. Marin, 53.

4. Randy Frame, "Sex Without Love," *Christianity Today* (April 22, 1983), 25.
5. Marin, 53.
6. Lewis B. Smedes, *Sex for Christians* (Grand Rapids, Michigan: William B. Eerdmans Publishing Company, 1976), 24.
7. Donald Nicholl, *Holiness* (New York: The Seabury Press, 1981), 46.
8. C. S. Lewis; source unknown.
9. Marin, 54.
10. Dwight Hervey Small, *Your Marriage Is God's Affair* (Old Tappan, New Jersey: Fleming H. Revell Company, 1979), 11-12.
11. Marin, 54.
12. Tim Timmons used the "balloon payment" metaphor in a lecture.
13. Frame, 25.
14. Rollo May; source unknown.
15. Peterson, *Five Smooth Stones for Pastoral Work*, 28.
16. Ben Patterson, "Dirty Jokes," *The Wittenburg Door* (April-May 1981): 3-4.

CHAPTER 10

1. For a more complete discussion of marriage as a covenant, see J.D. Douglas, ed. *The New Bible Dictionary* (Grand Rapids, Michigan: William P. Eerdmans Publishing Company, 1962), 267-268.
2. Archibald D. Hart, *Feeling Free* (Old Tappan, New Jersey: Fleming H. Revell Company, 1979), 85.
3. Smedes in a lecture.
4. Dr. David and Jan Stoop, *Refresh Your Marriage with Self Talk* (Old Tappan, New Jersey: Fleming H. Revell Company, 1984), 133.

CHAPTER 11

1. C. S. Lewis, *The Four Loves* (New York: Harcourt Brace Jovanovich, Inc., 1960), 169.
2. Eugene H. Peterson; source unknown.
3. John Powell, S.J. *Why Am I Afraid to Tell You Who I Am?* (Allen, Texas: Argus Communications, 1969), 88.

CHAPTER 12

1. David Augsburger, *Caring Enough to Confront* (Ventura, California: Gospel Light, 1983), 3.

CHAPTER 13

1. John Powell, S.J. *Why Am I Afraid to Love?* (Allen, Texas: Argus Communications, 1967), 24.
2. Tim Hansel quotes Paul Tournier on page 80 of *When I Relax I Feel Guilty*.

CHAPTER 14

1. Peck, 15.

Epilogue

1. Morris West, *The Shoes of the Fisherman* (Toronto: Bantam Books, Inc., 1963), 186.
2. Peterson, *Five Smooth Stones for Pastoral Work*, 49.
3. Margery Williams, *The Velveteen Rabbit* (New York: Avon Books, 1975), 16-17.

Bibliography

Bibliography

Augsburger, David. *Caring Enough to Confront*. Ventura, California: Gospel Light, 1983.

Douglas, J.D., ed. *The New Bible Dictionary*. Grand Rapids, Michigan: Wm. B. Eerdmans Publishing Co., 1962.

Frame, Randy. "Sex Without Love." *Christianity Today*, April 22, 1983, 24-28.

Hansel, Tim. *When I Relax I Feel Guilty*. Elgin, Illinois: David C. Cook Publishing Company, 1979.

Hart, Archibald D. *Feeling Free*. Old Tappan, New Jersey: Fleming H. Revell Company, 1979.

Howard, J. Grant, Jr. "Interpersonal Communication: Biblical Insights on the Problem and the Solution." Portland, Oregon: Western Baptist Press, 1976.

Lewis, C. S. *The Four Loves*. New York: Harcourt Brace Jovanovich, Inc., 1960.

Marin, Peter. "A Revolution's Broken Promises." *Psychology Today*, July 1983, 50-57.

Miller, Alice. *The Drama of the Gifted Child*. Translated by Ruth Ward. New York: Basic Books, Inc., 1981.

Miller, Keith and Andrea Wells Miller. *The Single Experience*. Waco, Texas: Word Books, 1981.

Nouwen, Henri J. M. *Making All Things New: An Invitation to the Spiritual Life*. San Francisco: Harper and Row, 1981.

Nicholl, Donald. *Holiness*. New York: The Seabury Press, 1981.

Patterson, Ben. "Dirty Jokes." *The Wittenburg Door*, April-May 1981, 3-4.

Peck, M. Scott. *The Road Less Traveled*. New York: Touchstone, 1978.

Peterson, Eugene H. *Five Smooth Stones for Pastoral Work*. Atlanta: John Knox Press, 1980.

_____. *A Long Obedience in the Same Direction*. Downers Grove, Illinois: InterVarsity Press, 1980.

Powell, John, S. J. *Why Am I Afraid to Love?* Allen, Texas: Argus Communications, 1967.

_____. *Why Am I Afraid to Tell You Who I Am?* Allen, Texas: Argus Communications, 1969.

Small, Dwight Hervey. *Your Marriage Is God's Affair*. Old Tappan, New Jersey: Fleming H. Revell Company, 1979.

Smedes, Lewis B. *Sex for Christians*. Grand Rapids, Michigan: William B. Eerdmans Publishing Company, 1976.

Stoop, Dr. David and Jan. *Refresh Your Marriage with Self Talk*. Old Tappan, New Jersey: Fleming H. Revell Company, 1984.

Tournier, Paul. *The Meaning of Persons*. New York: Harper & Row, 1957.

West, Morris. *The Shoes of the Fisherman*. Toronto: Bantam Books, Inc., 1963.

White, Mel. *The Other Side of Love*. Old Tappan, New Jersey: Fleming H. Revell Company, 1978.

Williams, Margery. *The Velveteen Rabbit*. New York: Avon Books, 1975.